Mary Tyler

# My Years in
# an Indian Prison

*with illustrations by Dilip Ray*

Penguin Books

Penguin Books Ltd, Harmondsworth,
Middlesex, England
Penguin Books, 625 Madison Avenue,
New York, New York 10022, U.S.A.
Penguin Books Australia Ltd, Ringwood,
Victoria, Australia
Penguin Books Canada Ltd, 2801 John Street,
Markham, Ontario, Canada L3R 1B4
Penguin Books (N.Z.) Ltd, 182–190 Wairau Road,
Auckland 10, New Zealand

First published by Victor Gollancz Ltd 1977
Published in Penguin Books 1978

Made and printed in Great Britain by
Richard Clay (The Chaucer Press) Ltd.,
Bungay, Suffolk
Set in Monotype Plantin

Penguin Books
My Years in an Indian Prison

Mary Tyler was born in Tilbury, Essex, in 1943. She
graduated in Modern Languages from King's College,
University of London, in 1965. After working as a
bookshop manageress, teacher and translator, she left
for India in December 1969 to visit Amalendu Sen,
a Bengali engineer whom she had met in West Germany,
and whom she married in April 1970. In May of the
same year they were both arrested on a variety of
charges which included conspiracy to overthrow the
Indian government. After more than five years spent
in Bihar prisons awaiting trial, the charges against
Mary Tyler were suddenly withdrawn. She was deported
from India but Amalendu Sen remained in detention.
Since returning to Britain, she has given many talks
in several countries and has written a number of articles
about the political situation in contemporary India.

For Dhatingna, Prokash and the other dear children of the jail, who, I hope, will live to see a brighter future. For those in India and elsewhere who are behind bars for a just cause. Lastly, for all those dear ones, too numerous to name individually, who trusted and helped me through the long years of imprisonment.

# Contents

*List of Illustrations*  9
*Author's Note*  11
1 Naxalite!  17
2 Solitary  31
3 A Political Prisoner  49
4 The Shooting  63
5 Companions  77
6 False Alarms  92
7 Repatriation?  103
8 Tata  119
9 Committal  134
10 Crisis  146
11 The Movement  161
12 Dhatingna  176
13 Last Transfer  190
14 A Ticket to London  200
*Postscript*  215

# Illustrations

Calcutta 1970   22
Hazaribagh Central Jail Female Ward   33
Hazaribagh Jail – inside my cell   40
Kalpana's cell and mine   51
Hazaribagh – watchtower   72
The Naxalite section at Jamshedpur   131
Inside the female ward   155

# AUTHOR'S NOTE

# The 'Naxalite' Movement

The word 'Naxalite' is derived from the village of Naxalbari in the Siliguri District of North Bengal, where, in the Spring of 1967, there took place an armed peasant uprising against the big landowners and usurers of the area. The ultimate aim of the uprising, which was led by members of the District Committee of the Communist Party of India (Marxist), at that time the dominant partner in the West Bengal United Front Government, was the seizure of state power. Attempts were made to overturn the whole power structure in the villages and to replace it by peasant committees; unjust debt and mortgage agreements with landlords and moneylenders were destroyed, and steps taken towards redistributing to poor and landless peasants, who formed 70 per cent of the population of the area, all land that was not owned by those who tilled it.

It is not the aim of this book to relate in detail or to attempt to analyse the subsequent development of the 'Naxalite' movement. The most important consequences of the Naxalbari uprising were the rapid spread of similar peasant struggles to other parts of India, the split in the Communist Party of India (Marxist), the leadership of which strongly opposed the Naxalbari line, and the forming, in 1969, of the Communist Party of India (Marxist-Leninist), which continued to spearhead the movement, though many of the people described as 'Naxalites' never in fact belonged to it. In 1970–71, the 'Naxalites' suffered serious setbacks, partly, in my opinion, because of various political errors, and partly as a result of the relentless and brutal campaign carried out against them by the Indian Government.

There is no group of people in India which calls itself 'Naxalite'. The term was coined by opponents of the movement as a derogatory description of its supporters. Later, it came to be used by other sections of the population in the same way in which I have used it in this book: to describe proponents of and sympathizers with a political trend which is not at the present stage confined to one single organized group of people. Broadly, the Naxalites regard the 1947 Independence as a sham and the ruling Congress Party as one which represents the interests of big landowners and the comprador bourgeoisie. They see India as a semi-feudal and semi-colonial country which can achieve true independence only through protracted armed struggle as there has been in China and Vietnam. They see the first stage of this struggle as being the fight for true people's democracy, the essence of which is agrarian revolution to eradicate feudalism.

As for myself, I lay no claim to any comprehensive knowledge about the Naxalite movement; by far the greater part of what I know was learned within jail walls. The Naxalites with whom I came into contact struck me as being sincere and honest, genuinely concerned with the well-being of the Indian people, patriotic and ready for self-sacrifice. I heard them praised by staff and prisoners alike for their courage, resistance to the prevalent corruption, selflessness and their ability to identify with the most downtrodden sections of the population. The survival of the Naxalite movement in the face of massive government repression is an indication of the relevance of its politics to the needs of the Indian people. Their rejection of Indian parliamentary democracy as a farce has been fully borne out by the events of 26 June 1975, and the now total inability of opposition parties to function in any effective way through the parliamentary system. Shortly after the declaration of 'National Emergency', all Naxalite groups were officially banned by the Congress Government. However, they had long been accustomed to clandestine work and continue to operate as before. Ultimately time alone will be the judge of whether the Naxalites can provide the political leadership which can solve India's problems.

I wish to emphasize that the word 'Naxalite', in the context of this book, should on no account be interpreted as having any derogatory connotations.

In order to protect people still in India, many things must, at this stage, remain unsaid. For the same reason, I have changed some names and transposed some events. I hope that one day, when India is a better place, the full story will be told. Those who helped me, and whom I have not mentioned, know why it must be so and will forgive me. The reader, I hope, will be generous enough to do the same.

*My Years in an Indian Prison*

# 1. Naxalite!

June 1970. I am sitting at a table brought to my cell in Hazaribagh Central Jail, Bihar, India. Facing me are six or seven plain-clothes police officers. Some lean forward, insistent, accusing, their faces hardly a foot away from mine. Others lounge back, seemingly relaxed and benign, basking in satisfaction with their catch; but their eyes remain fixed on me. The youngest is questioning me, his small red eyes sunk in a face puffy with excess, mouth set hard and cynical, expression frozen by daily familiarity with the interrogation routine.

'You are Chinese.'
'No, British.'
'I say you are Chinese. Where is your passport?'
'In Calcutta.'
'You are lying. I have your passport. Do you want to see it?'

They have seized it with my money and other belongings from my father-in-law's house in Calcutta. The stamps of countries I have visited on my overland journey to India puzzle them.

'You have been to China?'
'No.'
'Africa?'
'No.'

A couple of days later, the press in India and Britain reports that I have visited China, Japan and several African countries.

The Nepalese and Pakistani stamps particularly disturb my interrogators.

'You have been smuggling arms from China.'
'You have been sent to organize a revolution here.'

One so-called nationalist has an even stronger imagination.

'We got rid of the British Raj. Now you want to rule us again.'

For the umpteenth time I relate every detail of my past life; my father's name, my address, my employers, my whole itinerary, the name of every hotel I have stayed in since leaving England six months ago. Next comes the political interrogation.

'What do you think of China?'
'I admire it.'
'China is our enemy. Do you support North Vietnam?'
'The Vietnamese people have the right to decide their own affairs without foreign intervention.'
'What about North Korea?'
'I know very little about it.'

They tell the press that I am a Maoist, a dangerous communist revolutionary.

'What kind of gun did Amalendu have?'
'He was unarmed.'
'You are lying again. We have enough evidence to hang him.'
'Perhaps we shall have to twist her stomach and squeeze the truth out of her.'
'Can I see my husband? I want to arrange for a lawyer to come.'
'Who is your husband? You are not married. You are a casual wife to all the Naxalites.'
'And you are disgusting.'

'I apologize for his bad manners. Of course you can see your husband. Just write a petition.'

Next day, the newspapers report that I have asked to live with my 'unofficial' husband in jail. I do not see Amalendu again before leaving India five years later.

They check and re-check every detail.

'Why did you come to India?'
'To see the country and the people, to learn.'
'Why did you stay here?'

How could I explain to them the reasons for staying in India? As if they, defenders of the indefensible, would understand.

I had left my translating job in London at the beginning of December 1969, to travel overland to India on a six-month trip I had been planning and saving for. From my schooldays, influenced perhaps by the proximity to our home in Essex of Tilbury Docks, where my father worked and which at that time were always busy with shipping from distant parts of the world, I had been fascinated by foreign countries and people. From my early teens I had saved my pocket money to spend the summer holidays abroad. With adulthood and years at university in London and Germany that brought me into contact with students from five continents, I started to become conscious of how other nations regarded us, the British. I began to realize that the 'glorious' imperial history we had been told about in school was not something to be so proud of after all and to understand how the policies pursued by Britain and other colonial powers in their dominions overseas had in fact largely contributed to the present poverty of countries like India.

During the two years I spent teaching at a school in Willesden, North London, attended by pupils from many different countries, I developed an interest in the question of race relations, and spent some of my spare time working for the Campaign

Against Racial Discrimination. It was at about this time that I met Amalendu Sen, an engineering trainee working in West Germany, one summer when I was returning from a holiday in Germany. What started as a casual conversation in a train developed into a firm friendship based on a similar approach to political and social questions. At the end of 1967, Amalendu decided to return to his home in Bengal, East India; I respected his decision to forsake the comforts of life in Europe in order to try to make some contribution towards helping his country.

Amalendu wrote to me regularly from Calcutta, and some time later suggested that I take a few months off work to visit India and see things for myself. Accommodation would be no problem; his family would welcome me. Considering that such an opportunity should not be missed, I eagerly accepted his invitation, and, within six months, had saved enough money for the trip.

My parents had met Amalendu once, but were still perturbed by my intention of making an extended journey to a country so far from home. As I kissed them good-bye after my last weekend with them, instead of the usual words of warning, my father just said:

'You know, dear, you will probably see many appalling sights, but don't let them affect you too deeply; try to remain detached.'

Some paternal instinct perhaps told him that all the poverty, suffering and inhumanity I was likely to encounter in India might change me for ever.

Six weeks later, on 18 January 1970, after an interesting but unexceptional overland journey through Turkey, Iran, Afghanistan and West Pakistan, I was sitting in a third-class compartment of the Kalka Mail, speeding across the thousand miles between Delhi and Calcutta, looking forward to a reunion with Amalendu, whom I had not seen for two years, and wondering whether he would be able to accompany me to Darjeeling and maybe Sri Lanka. It was on this train journey that I had my first hint that all might not be as I had anticipated. A young naval officer who had helped me locate my seat came along to my compartment at intervals to chat to me. He warned me that Calcutta was a fearsome city, full of strife and turmoil, and that the State of Bengal had become ungovernable. Peasants had been looting crops from landlords' fields, and in the city warring political parties had taken law and order into their own hands. He advised me to make my stay there as brief as possible.

I had read the London newspaper reports of the 1967 Naxalbari peasant uprising in North Bengal and the movement that had developed from it; and had felt a stir of excitement at the possibility of revolution in India, a country so vast and populous that a radical change there could not but exercise considerable influence on the whole pattern of world politics. As the young officer talked, I listened with interest, though without comment. However, my concern, unlike his, was not for the landlords and their losses. I was thinking of the desperate peasants and the conditions of extremity that must have led them to loot the harvests.

Despite the dire warning I had received and my comparative familiarity with the situation in India, I was unprepared for Calcutta. On my first taxi ride from the station, littered with ragged and leprous humanity, every wall I passed hit me with yard-high slogans: *Political Power Comes from the Barrel of a Gun. Red Salute to Naxalbari. China's Path is Our Path.* Lamp-posts were hung with large maps showing the development of armed struggle in nearly every district of Bengal.

Amalendu's house was in an area populated by refugees from East Bengal, where his family had also originated. Like their neighbours, they had left their home after the partition of India and Pakistan in 1947. I spent the first few days getting accustomed to life in a Bengali household, meeting countless friends and relatives, and being regaled with all manner of delicacies. But it did not take me long to get used to the Special Branch police loitering in the shadows of shop doorways in the area and under the coconut palms by the pond in front of the house. Amalendu's elder brother made sure that there was nothing published in Peking among my books; Chinese publications had been seized and their owners arrested from near-by

houses. Later, a neighbour told me that he had even thrown his family's ancestral swords into the small water reservoir behind his house in case the police should conduct a raid and charge him with keeping offensive weapons.

Already in January it was warm, and I realized that if I wanted to travel south I would have to go before the weather got too hot. I decided to go to Puri, a seaside town in Orissa. After a few days' sightseeing in Calcutta I departed, promising to return in a month or two. Amalendu was not able to come with me as I had hoped, so I set off alone, on 25 January, by the Puri Express.

During the next two months I went from Puri to Madras, Sri Lanka, Bombay and Katmandu, seeing the usual places of interest, admiring temples, marvelling at ancient rock-carvings, lazing on tropical beaches. Often I joined up with other tourists for bus and car excursions, but somehow I always felt detached from them; I knew that I was not seeing India with the same eyes as they. Certain scenes impressed themselves upon me far more deeply than any historic monument, scenic wonder or technological achievement. In Benares, while fellow-tourists were exclaiming over the Golden Temple and the Maharajah's palace, I was still thinking about a notice I had read that morning beside the holy River Ganges: PHOTOGRAPHING OF BEGGARS, BATHERS, LEPERS, DEAD BODIES, ETC., IS STRICTLY PRO-HIBITED.

In Agra, I filmed the Taj Mahal almost as a duty, but after-wards what I remembered most about the city was the humilia-tion of the rickshaw cyclist, compelled by poverty to tail me for hours in the remote hope that I might hire him for a ride that would give him a few coins to buy flour and salt for his family. In Puri, I stood outside the sacred temple of Lord Jagannath, struck more by the sight of the lepers lining the streets that led up to it than by the temple itself. The tourist attractions of other cities, too, seemed unimportant beside the sight of a woman in an advanced state of pregnancy lying in the street ignored, another washing her saucepan in water flowing along a gutter, and, in Calcutta, a city where men are con-demned to a level of degradation as low as anywhere on earth, rickshaws pulled by skeletal, near-naked, barefoot runners, stumbling through mud and potholes.

It was not difficult to understand why India could be patient no longer, and I began to feel that what I had heard in those first days in Calcutta could really be the early rumbling of a volcano about to erupt. As the months passed, I felt less and less like a tourist as my concern for the beggars, the lepers, the poor, the discarded and humiliated deepened. In the end, the ancient history and culture of India came to have no greater meaning for me than it had for them.

On my return to Calcutta, I found the city in even greater turmoil. The United Front government had resigned and the State of Bengal was under President's rule. I went to the bank to change money, and found the clerks discussing the correct tactics of armed struggle in the countryside. Coffee houses in the city were thronged with students and intellectuals excitedly talking about the Naxalites' liberated zone of three hundred villages in Srikakulam, Andhra Pradesh. There was talk that there would soon be another liberated area in Midnapur, West Bengal. Large-scale round-ups of suspected Naxalites were still taking place in Calcutta itself.

There seemed to be general agreement among the Naxalite sympathizers I spoke to that the first aim of struggle in India must be to bring about land and social reforms in the villages where over 70 per cent of the population still lived, often in near-feudal conditions; consequently, there had been an exodus of educated youths to the countryside to propagate the politics of agrarian revolution and to join the peasants' struggles. When Amalendu's cousin took me to see one of the universities, I found little more than ghost buildings covered in slogans. Young people who had spent all their lives in the city were giving up home, comfort and education to share the hard life of the peasants, sacrificing themselves in the compelling urge to create a better India. I found among people I met a widespread sympathy for the Naxalites, inspired by a general and urgent desire for change, and a disillusionment with all existing parliamentary parties.

As the time drew near for my return to Britain, I discussed with Amalendu and others how I and other people concerned about India could best help her people. One day, one of his friends said, 'If you really want to help in some way, why don't you stay here with us?' The proposal was meant seriously, but seemed, at first, impracticable. I had my job, my flat and my family waiting for me in England. At the same time, affected as I was by the extremity of human suffering that I had seen, it seemed somehow a betrayal to return to the ease and comfort of life in London as if nothing had happened. After several days' reflection, I decided to stay on for the time being, at least until I had completed some further research and study of the Indian situation.

After his few years of European training, Amalendu had been offered a highly paid post that would have enabled him to live in comparative luxury. Instead, he had chosen to live a very simple life and spent much of his time with people living at the poorest levels of society. The luxury and extravagance he had seen abroad increased his concern for the plight of his own country. He always said that India would never be truly independent until all her people had sufficient food, clothing, housing, education and medical care.

After a few weeks spent together in Calcutta, he asked me to share this frugal life with him. The bond of affection that we already shared had been somehow strengthened by our mutual concern for the Indian people. We knew each other well; we shared the same principles and ideals, and Amalendu's family were already fond of me. I had, from the first, fitted well into their household, and felt quite at home. All the same, the decision to take such a big step was a difficult one. Days of mental conflict followed, but in the end I realized that the thought of returning to Britain and perhaps never seeing Amalendu again was too painful. Seeing him against the background of India, I admired more than ever his determination not to yield to the temptations of comfort and wealth. At last I was able to give him my answer, and on 10 April 1970, we married in the simplest Hindu ceremony. For us, this had no religious significance: it was the least complicated way of giving form to our intentions.

A few days previously, I had sat down to write the hardest letter of my life, to explain the situation to my parents who had been looking forward to my return. Naturally, they were hurt and disappointed, but my mother wrote saying that all they wanted was for me to be happy, and I must do whatever I thought right.

If I was to stay in India, I felt that the first thing I must do was to find out more about the villages, which were at the centre of all the present upheaval. Reading in journals about the continuing predominance of feudalism in the countryside, the never-ending debt of poor peasants to big landowners and moneylenders, bonded labour, the vast acreage of land owned by absentee landlords and farmed by sharecroppers, I realized that in all my travels I had learned very little of rural India. I had seen the monuments and palaces, coastlines and cities

25

proffered to visitors; I had walked in the slums and crowded urban bustees beloved of the doom-prophets of over-population. But until I was acquainted with the countryside, where most of the people lived, I could not claim to have seen India. I persuaded Amalendu to take me to an area where I could see for myself the reality of rural conditions. At the end of May we left Calcutta by train.

I had been in Singhbhum District – on the Bengal and Bihar border and not far from the steel city of Jamshedpur – only a couple of days when I was arrested. We were staying in a low hut of mud and thatch, the home of a poor peasant we had met on the way from the nearest bus stop several miles away. Most Indian villages are so isolated that there is no hotel or guest-house, but the people welcome strangers and willingly share whatever food they have. According to the Hindu religion, the guest is god. The village was inhabited mainly by tribal people who lived by subsistence farming. There had been a drought and it was hard to distinguish cultivated ground from uncultivated: all was dry and almost barren; the only plants to be seen were mint, weeds and forest shrubs. The area round the village was hilly and covered with trees. Just across the state border a few miles away was Midnapur, where the Naxalites had firmly entrenched themselves amidst a similar type of population. They had already penetrated some parts of Singhbhum but nobody in that particular village had heard of them. Apparently, however, the only man who appeared to own any amount of land in the village had been told to report the arrival of any newcomers to the police, and, although I was unaware of it, my presence was already known to them.

That morning, Amalendu and his younger brother had left early to walk to the nearest market town, about six miles distant, where they could get a bus into Jamshedpur. As they intended to return that same evening, I decided to stay behind in the village.

I was sitting under a thatched awning in the earthen courtyard in front of the house, dipping my hand into a bowl of rice cooked and steeped overnight in water. It had a sourish taste, complemented by the pungency of small raw onions. Women and children sat around staring at me, as they did at every mealtime, puzzled by my clumsiness in eating without knife and fork. The very effort of manoeuvring the rice into my mouth filled my belly, and I pushed the bowl away, still three-quarters full. The food made me sleepy and I asked to lie down on the wooden bed under the awning. Suddenly, someone was shaking me and gesturing to me to leave the house quickly. Dazed with sleep, I walked towards the gate she was pointing to. As I stepped on to the path outside, five armed police surrounded me, tied my neck, wrists and waist with ropes and started shoving me. Unable to breathe for the tightness of the rope around my neck, I motioned to them to loosen it. They took me to a clearing outside the village and made me sit under a tree. Red ants stung my thighs and buttocks. The sun burned hard upon my forehead and I felt dizzy. They were waiting for their officer to come from their camp in the jungle. They stood me up and searched me, taking away money, wristwatch, handkerchief and hairclips. Angrily, I shrugged off the hand that slid across my breast, and for the first time they realized that, despite my short hair and slacks, I was a woman. I sat down again; one of them, taking pity on me, gave me a swig of water from his bottle and wound a piece of cloth around my forehead. The officer arrived, arrogant and English-speaking. We began the hour-long march through the jungle, over rough and hilly paths strewn with stones and boulders. I was wearing only rubber sandals and soon my feet were cut and bleeding. The officer pushed me and urged me to hurry. I was reeling from the sun and the difficulty of negotiating the uneven tracks with my hands tied behind my back. When we were well clear of the village, the officer ordered me to stop. He wanted to search me. I told him they had already searched me in the village. He insisted that this time he was going to take off all my clothes and 'search me properly'. I warned him that I was a foreign national and he would lose his job if he laid a hand on me. I spoke more out of desperation than conviction, but it did the trick and he left me alone.

At the camp, senior officers were waiting, drinking Coca-Cola and eating biscuits. They asked me about my companions and, when I told them that I knew nothing, sent me down in a jeep to the police station several miles away in a village called Jadugoda. On the way, one of the armed constables told me he had had nothing to eat for two days. They had been combing the area for Naxalites, and their officers had not arranged any food supplies for them.

In the back room at the police station, armed men of the paramilitary Central Reserve Police lounged around leering at me. One of them was trying to catch my eye. I sat stiffly on a wooden bed. Numerous officers and civilians came and went, each repeating the same questions and each noting my replies in his little book. They asked me if I wanted a bath, and afterwards I realized they had been watching me through a crack in the door. They took me outside and photographed me. I was exhausted by the incessant questioning, but afraid to lie down on the bed. Through the open door I could see a boy sitting on the floor, his wrists handcuffed, waist roped, one eye purple and swollen, blood trickling down his cheek. He was wearing only shorts and shivering with fever.

They were going over the seizure list.

'Amalendu Sen, four hundred rupees.'

With a jolt I realized they had arrested Amalendu. I asked the next officer who came in to keep me together with Amalendu and take me away from these pointing and sniggering police. He ignored my request, but suddenly that evening they ordered me into the next room, where Amalendu, his brother and about fifteen others were sitting on the floor, roped together. We were given food; the men had only one hand untied to eat it. Afterwards they took Amalendu and several others away to the cells. The rest of us were left for the night. I lay down to sleep. The boy with the swollen eye was shivering again. He asked the officer to return his clothes and was answered with a sneer. I placed the cloth the policeman had given me around his shoulders. They had hit him with a rifle butt.

Next morning they took us to Chaibasa, district town of Singhbhum. They took away my sandals and all the men's clothing except shorts and vests. All day we sat in the stuffy police van without food and water. Some of the younger men were singing and joking. I sat talking quietly to Amalendu. Confident that I at least should be released soon, he told me, half in jest, to be sure to visit him in jail.

Three days in the prison at Chaibasa. The Jailer asked me if I was male or female and told the wardress to check my sex. I was conducted to the female ward. At night we were crammed together, the latrine stank and filled the hot dormitory to the point of nausea; the wardress, locked in with us, shouted and wielded her stick at some prisoners bedded at the far end of the dormitory near the latrine. In the morning she went off duty and a warder came in and lay on her bed. Some women fondled him, took off his belt, playfully hid his keys. I was still numb and too tired to care about what they were doing. Other women brought soap and oil, bathed me and massaged my bruised legs and feet, still sore after the forced march through the jungle.

On the third night Kalpana, an English-speaking Bengali girl of a middle-class family, arrived. She had been arrested the day after me, rounded up during the police combing and accused, like myself and the others picked up, of being a Naxalite. She was weary, able to speak only of the torture and beating she had seen during her two days at the police station. She told me that she had seen five men suspended by their wrists from the wall and beaten with rifle butts. Those who did not 'talk' after this had a rod inserted into the anus until they screamed. When not being interrogated, she had been locked in a tiny cell with about eighteen men.

Police interrogations continued in the Chaibasa Jail office. The intelligence officers were angry that the other women prisoners had lent me a change of clothing, annoyed that I was already developing a relationship with women with whom they had imagined I would not be able to communicate. Because they themselves were out of touch with the people, they did not understand that, even without a common language or culture, mutual sympathy can be established. The Jailer, lest any aspersion be cast on his authority, broke the glass bangles the women had put on my wrists and warned me against associating with 'thieves and murderesses', as he described them.

On Monday, 1 June 1970, we were transferred. Undeterred by the presence of a couple of dozen armed guards, I sat chatting to Amalendu, who told me we were going to Hazaribagh, 142 miles away. I had never heard of the place before. One of the men, who had been in preventive detention for two months once before, was telling us about prison life, the food we would get, and what we would have to wear. But neither of us seriously thought that we would be in prison for long. It was only after a couple of years in jail that I realized just how naïve we had been.

In the jail office at Hazaribagh, a clerk wearing pebble spectacles, furious at my attempt to follow Kalpana to the 'female' side of the room, ordered me to squat on the floor among the male prisoners. This raised a laugh, and, perplexed, he started asking me my caste, my father's name and all the same details yet again. Afterwards I said good-bye to Amalendu for the last time, no longer allowed to speak to him but able just to stroke the top of his head and smile at his brother as they crouched on the stone floor and Kalpana and I passed by to follow a warder through the small door set in a high wooden gate that opened on to the jail interior. It was dark. Guided by the warder's lantern, we walked barefoot along a stony path, past high walls, to another gate topped with iron spikes. We entered, and the gate slammed behind us.

## 2.  Solitary

At five-thirty next morning, the fifth after my arrest, I was aroused from a sleep of exhaustion by the 'matine' (the word 'mate' with the Hindi feminine ending), the trusted prisoner in charge of the female ward, who sent me and Kalpana out to join the dozen or so pairs of crouching women lined up outside the dormitory waiting to be counted by the Chief Head Warder. Heads covered, faces downturned, some clasping sleeping children, they waited, humble, silent and motionless, as the warder strutted along the line tapping each pair with his stick and checked the total against a crumpled scrap of paper in his hand. Resenting the matine's instruction to crouch down behind the other women, we remained standing. When the warder departed we had time to assess our new surroundings. At first sight, the female ward of Hazaribagh Central Jail looked pleasant enough; a long, low, yellow-ochre washed central dormitory, surrounded by an expanse of red earth bordered on two sides by a vegetable garden; paths from the gate to the dormitory and along by the right-hand wall edged with bushes of blossoming jasmine; a few trees, guavas, mangoes, lemon, margosa and bougainvillaea; the whole enclosed by twelve-foot walls of roughly hewn stone blocks in variegated tones of grey.

Before our exploration was complete, the gate opened once more and two male convicts in coarse white shorts and blue-striped vests, accompanied by another warder, entered at a trot to dole out the women's breakfast from two dirty-looking buckets. After sloshing the food into the women's waiting receptacles which were lined up on a low concrete wall just inside the gate, they ran out again. Mymoun, the matine, called us and gave us each a handful of raw chick peas and a sticky pellet of

31

gritty dark cane molasses in a half-litre aluminium tumbler and handed us a six-inch piece of stick to clean our teeth. Ravenous, I started cramming chick peas into my mouth, oblivious of the mud clinging to them and hardly aware of the horrified expressions of my fellow prisoners, according to whose customs it was unthinkable to touch food in the morning without having a wash and cleaning one's teeth. Years after, when I knew them much better, they never tired of reminding me of my uncouth behaviour on that first morning. Kalpana's stomach was more delicate than mine. She chewed a few chick peas individually and half-heartedly, then, longing for a cup of tea and unable to eat any more of this 'horse food', as she called it, she put down her tumbler on the lid of the water butt in the dormitory; the matine made a rush at us, swept away the tumbler and shrieked at her for contaminating the water. I was unable to understand the reason for this fury until Kalpana explained that, according to Hindu belief, half-eaten food is unclean. In fact the matine, as I later discovered, was a Muslim.

We resumed inspection of our new home, but within a few moments there was a general scuttling about and all the women dashed into the dormitory and formed a line along one side, heads covered with the ends of their sarees, eyes demurely downcast. Hastily, the matine pushed some pink plastic sandals under piles of khaki government uniforms lying on the floor. Months afterwards we understood why she had hidden them: footwear was not a part of jail issue and they had been purchased secretly from a warder.

The bell outside the gate clanged frantically, and as the gate swung open two officers of the jail entered, accompanied by the Chief Head Warder and several armed and khaki-clad guards. We became familiar with this type of retinue in the months to come; the Superintendent and Jailer never stepped among the prisoners without an armed escort. The wardress stood awkwardly to attention and saluted, her upswinging arm hampered by the folds of her heavy khaki saree. Kalpana and I had been placed by the matine at the far end of the line. The officers strode past the other women as if unaware of their existence.

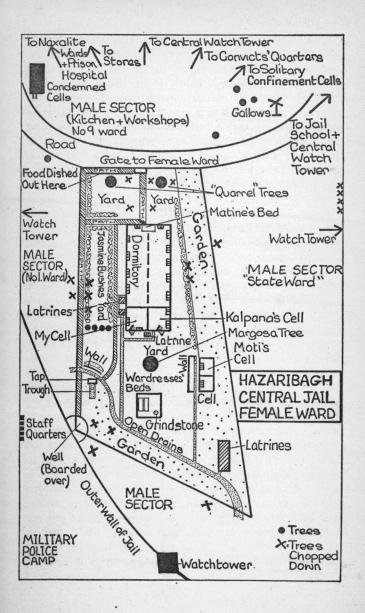

To Naxalite Wards + Prison Hospital Condemned Cells

To Stores

To Central Watch Tower

To Convicts' Quarters

To Solitary Confinement Cells

MALE SECTOR (Kitchen + Workshops) No 9 ward

Gallows

To Jail School + Central Watch Tower

Road

Gate to Female Ward

Food Dished Out Here

Yard

Yards

"Quarrel" Trees

Matine's Bed

PATH

Garden

Watch Tower

Watch Tower

MALE SECTOR (No.1 Ward)

Jasmine Bushes Yard

Dormitory

MALE SECTOR "State Ward"

Latrines

My Cell

Kalpana's Cell

Margosa Tree

Latrine Yard

Moti's Cell

Wall

Wardresses Beds

Cell

HAZARIBAGH CENTRAL JAIL FEMALE WARD

Tap
Trough

Wall

Staff Quarters

Grindstone

Open Drain

Garden

Latrines

Well (Boarded over)

Outer Wall of Jail

MALE SECTOR

MILITARY POLICE CAMP

Watchtower.

• Trees
X Trees Chopped Down

Halting in front of us, and without acknowledging our presence, they started giving instructions in Hindi to the wardress. The short stout man with dark glasses, the Jail Superintendent, finally wheeled towards us to ask whether we had anything to say. Kalpana had the presence of mind to ask for reading matter, soap and a change of clothing. There was no response. They departed as abruptly as they had come and immediately the wardress sent prisoners to clear out the blankets and utensils stored in two cells at the far end of the dormitory block. Kalpana had understood some of the conversation in Hindi and told me we were to be kept in solitary confinement.

By ten o'clock that morning I found myself locked in a room fifteen feet square and completely bare except for a small earthen pitcher and three tattered, coarse, dark grey blankets stiff with the grease and sweat of several generations of prisoners, which I folded to make a pallet on the stone floor. My cell formed one corner of the dormitory building and looked out on to a yard at the end of the compound farthest from the gate. The two outer walls were open to the elements; instead of windows, there were three four-foot wide openings barred from the floor to a height of eight feet. The door was fastened with a long iron bolt and heavy padlock; the walls, covered in patchy whitewash, were pock-marked high and low with holes of long-removed nails. In one corner a rickety waist-high wooden gate concealed a latrine, a niche with a raised floor, in the centre of which was an oblong slit directly over a cracked earthen tub. My latrine jutted out adjacent to the one serving the dormitory where the rest of the women prisoners slept. The open drains from both these latrines and Kalpana's ran past the two outer walls of my cell, filling the hot nights with a stench that made me retch. The crevices between the broken concrete and crumbling brickwork of the drains were the breeding grounds of countless flies and giant mosquitoes that, as if by mutual pre-arrangement, performed alternate day and night shifts in my cell to disturb my sleep and rest.

My first few days in 'solitary' were spent as in a dream,

punctuated only by the Chief Head Warder's morning and evening rounds to check the lock, the bustling appearance of the matine bringing food and water, or the wardress fumbling with her keys to let me out to clean my teeth or bathe. When the interrogations resumed, I almost welcomed the arrival of plain-clothes police officers, heralded by convicts carrying chairs and table, as a chance to talk to somebody, for, not knowing any Hindi, I was unable to communicate even my basic needs to the matine, wardress or warder. Even police brought a breath of the outside world into the stifling isolation of my cell.

By now I had learned to play the interrogation game, and readily and elaborately related all the details of my past life, knowing that they would serve only as accretions to the vast files of useless information cherished by intelligence services all over the world, and certain that nothing I was telling them could ultimately be of any practical use. They were most anxious to know if I was acquainted with any Naxalite leaders and what I thought of the movement in general. Faced with the task of stamping out what newspapers called the 'extremist challenge', they saw my presence in a Bihar village as proof that I was an important link in an arms-smuggling set-up or a delegate of some ill-defined international organization sent to instigate and give guidance to revolution in India. Even a telegram sent to me by friends in England offering assistance was transformed in their eyes into a 'mystery telegram' with 'revealing contents'; I, like almost every person they picked up on their daily raids and round-ups, was subsequently described to the press as a 'Naxa-lite leader'. It was, no doubt, a way of showing results to the Government, which was demanding that they suppress the Naxalite movement.

In the cell next to mine, Kalpana was undergoing the same interrogations. We were unable to see each other, but, at night, when all except the armed guards in the turret-like watchtowers set at intervals in the outer jail wall were sleeping, we stood by our bars shouting to each other till late at night about our day's experiences and observations. I did not imagine that the police would bother to keep me longer than a week or two. They themselves had admitted that they were not interested in detaining me, even the most pessimistic among them predicting that I should be released within three months. At that time I had no idea of the extent of the stir my arrest had created outside, or of the newspaper emblazoned with headlines describing me as a 'Guerrilla Girl' and containing far-fetched accounts of my capture in a jungle hideout and accusing me, variously, of having tried to blow up a uranium complex, engaging in a forest gun battle with police, and bombing a police station.

At last the interrogators departed, to return to Delhi, Patna, Calcutta and Punjab, where they would peruse their sheaves of precious intelligence, and I sank back into a world fifteen feet square, cut off even from those parts of the jail beyond my bars. It was only then that the events of the past fortnight had their full impact on me. Up till that time I had hardly been conscious of what was happening; it was as if my brain had set up its own protective mechanism to carry me over the shock. Now, in solitary, I had plenty of time to think. Strangely enough, I was not at all frightened. The fact that I fully expected to be released at any moment prevented me from worrying much about myself; my main concern was for my parents. I guessed they must have been informed about my arrest, and could imagine their distress. The thought of their anxiety for me upset me very much. In addition, I was apprehensive as to what would happen to Amalendu. The police who had interrogated me had told me that he was in far worse conditions than mine. However, there was nothing I could do except write a letter to my parents and press the authorities to allow me to see Amalendu as the interrogators had promised. Before long, with no conscious effort I had come to grips with the situation and accustomed myself to the daily routine and the characters who controlled my life.

At four thirty a.m. a discordant bugle reveille would be sounded from the central watchtower to awaken the warders who were to come on morning duty. Shortly after, a triple bell summoned the convicts to start their long day's work. Just after daybreak, the crunch and thud of the Chief Head Warder's heavy boots across the stony ground alongside the dormitory warned me that my sleeping hours were officially over. After heaving his bulky frame up the three steps to my cell and rattling the heavy padlock and bars to check that I was still securely fastened in my cage, he uttered the only words he addressed to me for weeks, the same every morning and evening: '*Ek admi. Tik hai na?*' (One person. All right?) Sometimes, in garbled Hindi I had parrot-learned from Kalpana during the previous night's illicit conversations, I asked him to let me out for exercise, bring me writing materials or arrange for me to see Amalendu, but he just looked at me out of puzzled and suspicious eyes in a mustachioed hound-like face and shook his head sadly, a lugubrious giant, incongruous in a woollen beret and starched khaki shorts that flared out to reveal massive legs. I understood that he was not sure how to deal with me, perplexed by the presence of a 'memsahib' instead of the type of prisoners he was used to. Occasionally, he would see fit to administer his universal panacea, reassuring Kalpana that we should soon be released; in our case, no doubt, he genuinely believed it. Probably in all his years of government service he had not seen 'educated' women kept in these conditions. After his evening lock-checking, well before dark, he would squint and peer long and intently into my cell, searching every nook for any forbidden object I might somehow have secreted. One day I found a frayed piece of string by the water tap outside and tied it across the bars to dry my clothes. He stared at it in silence for several moments before motioning to me to remove it. After confiscating it, he explained to Kalpana that it was against the rules to have string in jail. I felt like a reprimanded schoolgirl.

Behind the Chief Head Warder on his evening rounds tripped Mymoun, the matine, at once servile and self-important, saree draped over her head, lips curved in a coy smile, face permanently uptilted to receive instructions from above, hands joined as if in prayer. She obviously wanted to make it clear to us that she was part of the establishment. In fact she was the purveyor of tales to the authorities and the executrice of their whims. Unlike the other women we saw, she was fat, smooth-skinned and neatly dressed. The source of her prosperity was soon revealed to us. She used to steal and sell the rations entrusted to her for the other prisoners, and, as we became increasingly aware from the daily diminishing portions served up to us, ours as well; everything allotted to us passed through her hands. Angered by her cunning, I thought of reporting her to the Jailer; Kalpana restrained me, pointing out that Mymoun too was a prisoner. It would be wrong on our part to compound her dishonesty by a betrayal of the unity between fellow-sufferers. Moreover, we could not afford to incur the enmity of Mymoun and the wardresses, whose goodwill alone could bring about any relaxation of the rules or easing of the severity of our conditions. So, though resentful of this petty thieving, we decided to keep quiet about it; why pick quarrels with the small fish when the sharks are waiting to devour you all?

Most of the responsibility for the female ward was left to the matine and decisions were taken by the Chief Head Warder. Between these two, the three wardresses were little more than custodians. They were locked with the prisoners in the female section, a kind of jail within a jail, and could not leave until a warder opened the gate from outside. They had been instructed to keep us under observation night and day, and so they spent most of their duty hours in the hut across the yard from our cells. Overcome by boredom and inertia, they frequently dozed off or lay for hours on the wooden bed surrounded by their favourite prisoners, gossiping about their families, the other wardresses, the rest of the jail staff and the prisoners. Their favourite occupation, it seemed, was to be massaged with mustard oil. Despite all orders forbidding them to talk to us, curiosity sometimes overcame them and they came to exchange a few words with Kalpana. They were all very poor, and their conditions of service little better than slavery. They rarely had a day off, and even when supposedly off duty, were obliged to remain on call inside the jail compound. They even had to obtain permission from the Chief Head Warder to go shopping. We often saw them being bullied, not only by the jail officers, but by their male counterparts, the warders, as well. They seemed to feel sad at keeping us locked up day and night, and sometimes one of the bolder ones used to unlock our cells and allow us to talk for an hour or so.

During the daytime, the key to the gate of the female ward was in the custody of a 'duty-warder', one of the 150 warders in the jail. He was responsible for opening the gate to admit convicts bringing food, the doctor or other persons on essential business. Administration of the jail was in the hands of a staff of Assistant Jailers and clerks, subordinate to the Jailer who had overall responsibility for the day-to-day running of the prison. He was answerable to the most exalted personage in the jail hierarchy, the Superintendent. With his dark glasses, solar topee and jacket covered in huge red checks, the Hazaribagh Superintendent would have looked more at home on a film set than in jail. He reminded me of a cross between an old-time film producer and a big game hunter. A member of the Westernized upper classes, he had spent some years in Canada, where he had picked up the phoney American accent that he invariably forgot halfway through a conversation. His unpredictable temper and behaviour were a source of as much exasperation to his subordinates as to ourselves. He demonstrated his authority by reversing his previous instructions so many times that in the end nobody was really sure what he wanted. The jail staff operated by by-passing him as much as possible so as not to get caught out if he happened to change his mind.

The monotony of those early days was often interrupted by his sudden and unannounced arrival, sometimes accompanied by police officers or members of the local elite come to inspect his new inmates. The wardresses lived in dread lest the advent of the 'sahib' should catch them in some unwitting infringement of his instructions. One day the little daughter of one of the prisoners came to give me two pink roses she had picked from the bushes just inside the gate. Delighted by the friendly gesture and the touch of fragrance and colour in my dreary cell, I stood them in my water tumbler.

That afternoon, the Superintendent chose to appear, and noticed the flowers as he passed my cell. 'You child of an ass!'

he roared at the wardress, summoning her as if beckoning a dog to heel and demanding to know where I had got the roses from. She was dumbstruck. Accusing her of allowing me to talk to other prisoners and ignoring my attempt at an explanation, he suspended her from duty forthwith. Indignant at the injustice, Kalpana and I decided to go on hunger strike until she was reinstated. She was allowed to resume duty next day. After this incident the wardresses realized that we did not want to cause them trouble and would, in fact, stand up for them; they became even more kindly disposed towards us, though were still constrained from exercising too much liberality by fear of losing their jobs.

Every time the Superintendent came, we accosted him with the same request: to be kept together in one cell. His barked reply never varied. 'Definitely not. You are Naxalite leaders. You want to be together so you can plan your escape and engage in conspiracies against the Government.' We found the notion of ourselves as important leaders amusing, but a hindrance to the programme of study we wanted to carry out together instead

Hazaribagh Jail - Inside My Cell

of wasting whole days in idleness, trying to occupy ourselves with the few possessions we had accumulated; an aluminium dish and tumbler, a comb and hand mirror, a couple of medicine bottles and two lengths of coarse cream cloth, jail-made sarees. In the mornings I spent half an hour rubbing my teeth with a piece of stick, one end chewed into a fibrous tuft, that served me as a brush. After eating I would wash my dish with water from the pitcher and spend a long time polishing it with the corner of a saree till it shone. I combed my two-inch hair time and again and paced the cell reciting all the poems I could remember. I devised exercise routines, but was hampered by severe dysentery and the lack of resilience in the stone floor that made my joints ache. Despite many pleas, we were allowed no writing materials, but received a heavily-censored newspaper that arrived smeared with greasy black ink. This we shared, and every time we wanted to pass it from one to the other we had to call the wardress. After a couple of days we found we could push it through the slit in the wall of Kalpana's latrine without troubling anyone. One day, Mymoun happened to notice us doing this. Next morning, male convicts arrived to nail a board across the aperture. The nails crumbled the surrounding plaster and the board fell off again within a couple of hours.

Apart from the newspaper, our only reading matter consisted of books from the jail library. I chose a Boswell's *Life of Johnson* and a volume of Shakespeare from the catalogue and looked forward to their arrival with pleasure. Disillusion awaited me. The brittle yellow pages were rendered illegible by the perforations of countless bugs, whose blood smeared every page. They crawled out of the books into my blankets, and I grew accustomed to their peculiar smell and transparent colouring that turned chestnut as they grew fat and bloated on their diet of my blood.

The high spot of each day was 'bathtime', when I was allowed to walk twenty yards from my cell to the one and only tap, suspended over a long cement trough. The water flowed for a couple of hours morning, noon and evening. All the other prisoners were locked up while I 'bathed' under the eyes of the wardress, dipping my aluminium tumbler into a bucket hung on the tap, and dousing myself as I squatted on the burning concrete slab alongside the trough. The water came through overground pipes that ran along the same gutter as the sewage from the men's ward next door, and in summer was always hot. After washing in a hot wind in the full glare of the midday sun, surrounded by the stink of sewage, and walking back barefoot across the hot sand to my cell, I felt parched and not in the least refreshed. A wardress showed me how to clean my clothes by banging them on the concrete slab; I had no change of clothing except the two lengths of cloth, which I wound around me until my slacks and T-shirt dried. Frequently I had to face officials clad only in this unlikely garb, but, in keeping with the strangeness of my whole situation, felt no embarrassment. Once I did ask the Superintendent for a blouse, but he said he could not see the need for one, as I was to be released very soon.

Late at nights, tired of shouting to Kalpana, I would stand in silence by the bars and contemplate the moon rising clear and serene above the *peepul* trees beyond the jail's outer wall; I watched a white owl perched motionless on the roof of the men's dormitory next door, frogs that leaped around the gutters and the tall margosa tree, home of a thousand sleeping birds, that stood in the yard outside my cell, and I felt that, in a strange world filled with a language I did not understand and situations beyond my comprehension, Nature at least was something familiar and tangible; I was grateful that imprisonment had not entirely cut me off from her.

From the early days we learned that every improvement in our conditions would be achieved only after doing battle with the inertia, unwillingness or inefficiency of the jail authorities. Never having set foot inside a jail before, neither Kalpana nor I had more than a vague notion of prison regulations. Probably my schoolmistress's love of order prompted me to ask to see the Jail Manual. The response to my innocuous request infuriated me. There was only one copy of the Jail Manual. That could not be spared. The rules said it had to remain in the jail office. No, I could not be permitted to go there and read it. If the jail was run by the rules I would not like it. Finally, the Jailer came out with it: the Jail Manual did not exist. It was out of print, the jail was run by memory. Not having access to any written rules, it was impossible to be sure of our rights or to know which of our needs and demands could be legitimately fulfilled. The attitude of most of the jail staff was that everyone in jail must have committed some crime to be there in the first place and it was a favour on the part of the government, as personified by themselves, to provide any food and shelter at all. People wanting to know rules and talking about 'rights' were nothing but a damned nuisance. Nevertheless, we were faced from the start with situations where we had no option but to come into conflict with the authorities; if we set a precedent of putting up with unreasonable conditions, they would inevitably take advantage of it.

Every day at about noon, the matine shoved a dish of food under the barred door and motioned to me to eat. It was the same every day; soggy rice mixed with stones and paddy husk, blackish-green water concealing a few lentils, and five or six pieces of potato complete with speckled skin and coated with a slimy sauce made from the water the rice had been cooked in, chillies and turmeric. One day it looked particularly unappetizing. The dish was leaking and black water trickled across the stone floor. I was trying to bring myself to touch it when Kalpana in the next cell called to me not to eat it. We decided to go on hunger strike until the quality of the food improved. Three days later, when the Jailer eventually came, it was decreed that Kalpana could have meals from the Naxalite section, where there had already been a hunger strike over food, and I, still suffering from dysentery, would receive mine from the jail hospital. Next day I fished out fourteen whole chillies from my portion of lentil soup and kept them to show the doctor, who seemed indifferent to my complaint that this was not the best diet for a sensitive digestion.

A few days later, the men arrested in the same round-up as ourselves tried to send us a message in the food sent for Kalpana. Mymoun, hiving off her usual share before passing it on to us,

43

discovered the letter folded in between some *chapatis*. After that, it was decided that we should cook our own food. We would be let out for a couple of hours on alternate days to do this. We were jubilant, knowing that official sanction to the opening of one of our cells, even for a limited period, was a major breakthrough.

Our weekly rations, consisting invariably of rice, coarse brown flour, red lentils, potatoes, a few onions, a little mustard oil and a handful of chillies and turmeric, were delivered to us on Sundays. We were given nothing to keep them in but managed to get two sacks from the Warder to cover the little mountains in the corner of Kalpana's cell. Once a week we were given a small quantity of sinewy and strong-smelling goat's meat that remained as tough as leather even after hours of boiling. Some concessions were forced upon me on the grounds of my European birth. Despite petitions to the contrary, I was issued with a finer grade of rice, a small quantity of tea and sugar and a little extra oil; these, however, were mere trifles in comparison with the royal treatment stipulated for European prisoners in accordance with jail rules devised by the British to suit themselves at the time of the Raj and unchanged by the Indian Government even after Independence. The convict in charge of the stores was a wild-looking fellow with black tousled ringlets down to his shoulders. He made a good profit in his position of influence in the jail, with so many saleable commodities at his fingertips, and often brought the matine some titbit or other he had managed to pick up.

'Cooking' henceforth became an important item on our daily agenda. We concocted every possible device to prolong our cooking time so that one of us could remain outside. The absolute minimum of time and effort was spent on the actual cooking process; we just boiled up our rice, lentils and potatoes in one saucepan for hours on end until they were a soggy gruel. If the wardresses became impatient we would explain that we were making 'English' food that took a long time to cook. We drank endless tumblers of weak and milkless tea, becoming accustomed to the metallic tang of aluminium in everything we consumed.

We spent the hours in seemingly inexhaustible conversation. Within a couple of weeks I knew more about Kalpana's life and she about mine than did members of our own families. More important, I was able to learn much from her about Indian customs and culture. Her presence eased my path through those first torturous months; explaining, translating, restraining my temper with endless patience, she helped me to gain acceptance with women who had never seen a European before. I don't know what I would have done without her.

The monsoon season brought difficulties. It rained nearly every day. The afternoons were black with terrific tropical downpours and howling winds. Each storm left our cells flooded, our blankets sodden, and ourselves crouched in a corner with nowhere dry to sleep. The Superintendent permitted us to tie jute mats across the upper half of the bars, but insisted that the lower part remain uncovered for the wardresses to maintain their constant vigil on our activities. Consequently, the rain streamed in unabated. It took repeated attempts to light the coal fire on which we had to cook, and sometimes we stayed hungry till late at night in the rain and wind till one of us managed to cook two black-streaked, half-raw *chapatis* tasting of smoke. Despite all this we welcomed the rain for the additional freedom it gave us. No officer ever ventured out in those downpours, so we were assured of a few hours' relaxed and uninterrupted conversation. We would sit, one inside her cell, the other on the ledge outside, with the rain dripping down on us through the jute matting. The wardresses thought we were crazy but after being in solitary confinement for several weeks we were eager to grab every opportunity of talking. We discussed what we would do when taken to court, planned our defence, composed speeches from the dock with an indefatigable optimism.

Several times we heard rumours that we were to go to court, but each time the given date passed with no greater event than a walk to the jail office to stand before the local magistrate, fat and complacent, and hear him profess himself helpless; he had no jurisdiction in our case, as we had been arrested in a different district. The walks to the office, however, brought a welcome

45

change in our routine, and, for me, a lurking, but unfulfilled hope that I might somehow see Amalendu. One day we did meet one of the men rounded up at the same time as ourselves. He urged us to demand political prisoner status; this, if granted, would give us far better facilities. Kalpana and I wrote petitions, but in fact were not sure whether we really should ask for any different treatment from the other women prisoners, as we feared it might irrevocably alienate us from them. We need not have worried. The Superintendent pronounced that we were criminals and would continue to be treated as such.

On the first of our outings to the office we asked the magistrate for details of the charges against us. He quoted four sections of the Indian Penal Code. We were, jointly with fifty other persons (all those who had been arrested in the same area at the same time as ourselves), accused of rioting with deadly weapons, causing an affray, armed robbery and attempted murder. The only thing I remember feeling was relief that the maximum sentence for the said offences was ten years! After a few weeks, the visits to the magistrate ceased, and he renewed our warrants without even seeing us. This was the government's interpretation of its law that an arrested person shall be produced before a magistrate within twenty-four hours of arrest and every fifteen days thereafter.

I had been held incommunicado for over a month before a British consular official from the Deputy High Commission in Calcutta was permitted to see me. He had already been fully instructed by the Indian authorities with their own version of events, and inquired little further from me than whether I was in good health and getting enough to eat. He informed me that permission would have to be obtained from Patna, the state capital, for me to have the change of underclothing I requested. The thought of my petition for underclothes being presented in writing to the Chief Secretary of the Bihar Government appealed to my sense of humour.

The consul was unresponsive to my request to meet Amalendu. The Indian authorities were disputing the validity of my marriage. This was nothing more than a ploy to prevent me from consulting with Amalendu, and, without seeing him, there was little I could do about it. Back in my cell, I paced back and forth pondering over the whole course of the meeting, furious that nothing serious had been achieved or even discussed. Some months later, another consul put the official line quite bluntly to me: what went on in India had nothing to do with me, and I must forget any principles I might have and concentrate on getting out of jail. After that first meeting, at which a horde of Special Branch policemen were present, the newspapers published a detailed account of my apparel and the praise I had allegedly given to the Indian authorities' treatment of me.

Shortly after this, I was overjoyed to receive my first letter; it was from a group of anonymous schoolchildren and assured me of their support and gratitude for my assistance in helping India along the right path. In view of my later bitter experience with correspondence, I now wonder how such sentiments ever managed to pass the censor. On the same day, Kalpana had a letter from a lady in Madras professing to be writing on behalf of a 'high-born gentleman' who would like to marry one or both of us (both our names had been published in newspapers) on condition that we were 'beautiful and under twenty-five'! We were not sure whether this was meant seriously or not, but for a joke asked the Warder for a letter form and replied asking for more details. It was perhaps just as well that we heard no more.

We longed to find out more about the other prisoners, but all contacts were furtive and fraught with danger, for women caught venturing too near our cells were scolded and sometimes beaten by the matine and wardresses. Still some magnetism drove the bolder ones towards us; they would appear like shadows by our bars in the hot afternoons when nearly everyone was resting. Though I could conduct no meaningful conversation with them, I was touched by the concern and sympathy I sensed in their expressions. At night one of them, a stocky peasant girl, used to bring my oil lamp. As she placed it on the floor just inside the door she would give me a quick smile and grimace in the direction of the matine, who had forbidden her to talk to me. I began to save half the orange the doctor had prescribed for me to slip into her hand as she came inside the cell. Hiding it in the folds of her saree, she would flee to the latrines to eat it in secrecy, out of sight of the matine and wardresses. From Kalpana's talks with the prisoners, we learned that most of them were awaiting trial; many had been there several years already. Several of them had young children, too small at the time of arrest to be separated from their mothers, but growing up in jail. These were the source of my greatest happiness; despite the admonitions of their elders, they were irresistibly attracted to my cell. Clambering up on the ledge in front of my bars, they would ask me to plait their hair, or demand to look in the mirror or try my glasses on. I used to entertain them with toys made from bent sticks taken from the broom I had been given to sweep my cell, and saved bits of my food for them.

After three months of partial solitary confinement, I had given up hope that the Superintendent would ever let us share a cell. I even devised a kind of motto for myself: 'Do not give the authorities the satisfaction of depriving you by yearning uselessly for what they will not give. Make your own alternatives.' Then, one September morning, as he was strolling past my cell, the Superintendent asked casually, as if it were a new suggestion coming from him, 'Would you two like to spend the days together?' There was no need of reply. The next morning our cells were unlocked and we were allowed out into the daylight and a new era of 'freedom'.

# 3. A Political Prisoner

The first day we were unlocked from dawn to dusk coincided with the departure of Mymoun. This was a relief to us; it was becoming increasingly difficult to keep quiet in the face of her cunning and bullying of other prisoners. The manner of her going was unexpected. When, after a delay of six years, her trial finally started, it was discovered that one major prosecution witness had died and another could not be traced. For lack of evidence, the judge was obliged to acquit both her and her husband, with whom she had jointly been accused of abducting the young woman who had subsequently become her co-wife, and who had also been held in custody pending the trial.

Mymoun's successor was Nago, a young woman of twenty-two or three, who had been in prison for some years and had several more of her seven-year sentence for attempted murder to serve. The authorities usually chose long-term convicts for positions of responsibility, encouraging them with the inducement of remisssion for good work. In effect, the government had in the matines and their male counterparts, the mates, a class of employees, able to earn money and 'bonuses' in the form of remission and various perks, in return for satisfactory and loyal service. Although Nago exercised the same petty tyranny over the other prisoners as her predecessor, she was cautious in her dealings with us, aware that, now that we were unlocked all day and could see what went on in the rest of the female ward, we were a potential source of trouble.

After three months confined to a cell, the compound seemed an exciting place. Left largely to our own devices, we spent most of the time in the open air. As the weather grew colder my health improved and the clear autumn days filled me with energy.

Sometimes Kalpana and I walked almost non-stop from five-thirty in the morning until the noonday sun drove us back into the cool of the cell; as we completed round after round of the compound we swung our arms and sang, as if we were on a country hike. In the afternoons we used to sit under the guava trees. Kalpana was keen to learn German and I was trying to learn Hindi and Bengali. We had no materials for study, but used twigs to write in the red dust.

As the female section of Hazaribagh Jail was theoretically only for short-stay prisoners awaiting trial, there was not a great deal of work to do. In the mornings the women used to sew buttonholes in government uniforms made in the tailoring workshop in the male section. After that they spent the time cleaning the dormitory, gardening, cooking or just talking. There was a peculiar system in Hazaribagh whereby prisoners received their daily lentils and vegetables ready cooked but were given raw rice and flour each morning. This they had to prepare as best they were able; no fuel or utensils were provided. They could obtain coal by sacrificing a day's food but had to cook in the same aluminium dish in which they collected their cooked food.

Now that we were allowed outside, we often sat chatting to our fellow-prisoners. I was unable to understand much of the conversations, and, though Kalpana translated, I felt I must make an effort to learn Hindi as quickly as possible.

Sometimes towards evening the younger women would start singing village songs and dance in rows. We learned several folk dances. They started off simple and repetitive, then, just when I thought I had mastered the steps, I would suddenly find myself dragged off in a series of leaps and skips that left me quite lost, much to the amusement of the onlookers.

But there was another side to life. As the winter approached, all the prisoners began to suffer from the lack of adequate clothing and blankets. Kalpana and I missed in particular the sandals that had been taken from us on our arrest and never returned. As the dry cold intensified, our feet split and bled. Most of our fellow-prisoners had never owned any sandals, but their toughened soles, too, cracked and became sore. As the stony

Kalpana's Cell and Mine

ground hardened, the children often cried from the cold and throbbing pain of wounds that would not heal. We were unable to continue our morning walks and exercise. We had to devise some footwear.

Having settled on a plan, we persuaded one of the wardresses, whom we had noticed to be particularly kindhearted, to lend us a pair of scissors, saying we wanted to cut our hair. The poor woman was horrified when we cut a strip from the end of one of our blankets, but we assured her that, if she kept quiet, nobody in authority would even notice. Sandwiched together with layers of newspaper and cardboard, and furnished with long laces of gauze obtained on some pretext from the prison hospital, the soles cut from the blanket made effective, if bizarre, espadrilles. For a time we were able to resume outdoor activities. We had, of course, asked the jail authorities to supply footwear, but as we were not classified as political prisoners we were not entitled to any, even though the winter temperatures in Hazaribagh are sometimes only a few degrees above freezing at night.

It was in November 1970 that we discovered what it really meant to be a 'political prisoner'. One night, unexpectedly, I was ordered to vacate my cell and go to join Kalpana. I was only too pleased to comply, happy at the thought of company. Excited by the surprise bonus and wondering what was happening, we sat watching as male prisoners passed our bars bearing a bed, mattress, blankets, pillows, a table and chair, cooking utensils and other items indistinguishable in the darkness. Later that night a new inmate arrived to occupy the cell that had been mine.

Next morning, the Chief Head Warder came, counted us, and went, and the new prisoner was still sleeping. Gazing like curious children through the bars, we glimpsed the corner of an expensive blue saree under a mosquito net. We were intrigued to make the acquaintance of this new type of prisoner. Later that morning, we talked to her. She was the secretary of a coalminers' union and had been arrested in connection with the murder of a mine manager at the Kedla colliery, about twenty miles from Hazaribagh. It struck me as ironic that this obviously rich woman in all her finery should be the representative of those ragged skeletons who spent their days in the damp tunnels beneath the earth in notoriously dangerous conditions. This exquisite lady gave the impression of being at the opposite pole of humanity from the workers whose interest she professed to have at heart.

As far as the authorities were concerned too, she was a creature far removed from the rest of us. She spent her days confined, not within our walls, but in social intercourse with the upper echelons of the jail staff in the office, never returning to her cell before nine or ten at night. Every morning she compiled a long shopping list of her requirements, which were duly purchased from the market and delivered before noon. Expensive Western foods and Indian delicacies were essential items of her daily diet. Costly garments were tailor-made to suit her fancy, countless pairs of sandals brought from the bazaar for her to choose from. These were her dues, befitting her status as a 'political prisoner'.

She commanded several servants from among the female prisoners. They worked from dawn till dusk fulfilling her demands, and she appeared to have no reservations about making them perform the most personal tasks. One morning I saw to my disgust that a young prisoner was washing her bloodstained sanitary cloths. The women delegated to work for her received no payment. As they had not been tried, their work was, in theory, 'voluntary', though they would not have dared refuse. As hardly 10 per cent of the whole jail population had been tried and convicted, most labour performed in jail was of this same type. Later, as conditions worsened and the prisoners became more militant, some forms of payment such as increased food rations were introduced.

Within a fortnight, the Political Prisoner had filled her cell with supplies of food, clothing, and household equipment, all provided by the government. She consumed considerable quantities of milk, meat, eggs and chicken, all of which are considered luxuries among the majority of Indian people and are rarely seen at all inside jail. When, after less than three weeks, she was released on bail, she took all her newly acquired possessions with her, leaving only a few potatoes for one of the wardresses. She left for the office followed by a line of convicts bearing her spoils, like an explorer of old with his retinue of bearers.

The Political Prisoner came from a wealthy family and, having political ambitions, saw trade union leadership as a stepping-stone to power. Some time later we read in the paper that she had become a Member of the Bihar Legislative Assembly; by then she had changed her affiliation from the Socialist to the Congress Party to suit the needs of the moment. Due, I suppose, to wealth and influence, the murder charge against her was 'forgotten'.

However she rendered us one service that I shall not forget. Despite our differences, she was conscious of the injustice of keeping us in prison without trial. Understanding this, I thought that she might be persuaded to help us. One day, I hesitantly approached her to give us some writing materials, which we were still sadly missing. Reluctant actually to defy the Superintendent's instructions, she nevertheless gave me the go-ahead to 'steal' a pencil and paper she would leave on her table when she next went to the office. This 'theft' was duly accomplished.

The Political Prisoner was the prototype of several I saw in the years that followed. They were treated with indulgence and deference by the jail staff, who were uncomfortably aware that, in the ebb and flow of the type of politics prevalent in India, those now in custody might one day be in power. Some warders even assured us that they would serve us too when we formed a government. It is often thought that the prison service attracts undesirable characters with a lust for power, but in India it is seldom so. In a situation where jobs are extremely hard to find, motivation is generally reduced to a single factor: economic necessity. Most of the prison staff were there simply because they needed the money. Prison service did, of course, arouse the brute instincts of some of the staff. In order to keep their jobs, they had to carry out orders from above however tyrannical these might be, but I only ever came across a handful of warders who actually enjoyed making difficulties and bullying prisoners. A few warders were genuinely sympathetic towards us, and when on duty would come to chat and give us news. One particularly liked me and I used to look forward to his duty, knowing that he would give me word of Amalendu, who, though he was separated from me only by a few walls, might as well have been a thousand miles away. One day this warder told me that Amalendu's mother had been to visit us but had neither been allowed to see me nor to leave the clothing she had brought for me.

As the months passed, it became obvious that our stay in jail was going to be far more prolonged than we had anticipated. There were rumours that our trial would start after the Durga Puja holidays in October, but all the festivals passed and nothing happened. Difficulties in our daily life mounted. If we wanted to write a letter home, it took five or six days of asking before we could obtain a letter form. We had to remind the Warder repeatedly for regular supply of our rations. Censorship of newspapers continued, requests for writing materials were still ignored. Our improvised footwear had worn out and the cold ground gave us pains in the legs. Several times I stumbled on bricks and stones and cut my feet open. Sleeping on the cold stone floor made our joints ache, and in the daytime we could not bear to sit inside the cell, where the winter sun never penetrated. Outside, the wind and dust plagued us and dried our skins till they resembled crocodile leather. Still, in comparison to most of the other prisoners, we were lucky. Kalpana's mother had brought us some clothes. Many of the women had barely a single thin garment to protect them from the harsh winter winds and spent the nights shivering under a couple of ragged blankets. The poor quality and meagre quantity of the lentils and curry dished up to them had long appalled us.

By the beginning of December, we had decided that we should have to go on a prolonged hunger strike. Demands were to cover both our own needs and those of the other prisoners. The Jailer told us that hunger strike would serve no purpose, but, on seeing our determination, he ordered the Warder to lock us in separate cells. We fasted for five days and nights, during which time we saw nobody except the doctor, the Chief Head Warder and the wardresses. On the morning of the sixth day, one of the office clerks turned up in front of my cell with a pair of pink plastic sandals for Kalpana and a beige rubber pair for me. Kalpana grimaced at the sight of those he had chosen for her but I urged her not to be fussy; at least one of our demands had been met and it was likely that others would be too. Later that day, it was agreed that clothing would be supplied to all the prisoners, and the quantity of food would improve. Censorship would continue and, as far as expediting our trial was concerned, the jail authorities insisted that this matter was not in their hands. They advised us to write a petition to the magistrate of Dalbhum, the sub-division where we had been arrested.

Judging that our hunger strike could achieve no more, we gave up, though we had already realized that jail petitions were dished out as palliatives for prisoners' grievances, and, even if dispatched or read, were never acted upon. They did, however, serve one useful purpose: by asking for a petition form every week I was able to obtain a pen for an hour or so. I would empty the ink into one of my medicine phials, and use it at night for writing stories, observations or poems by the light of the oil lamp. My paper supply was obtained from tea packets, the fly-leaves of library books, and the notebook in which I signed for the weekly rations; my pen was a thin stick taken from the broom.

After our hunger strike, even the heavily censored newspaper we had been receiving was stopped for a month as punishment, but the other prisoners were at least given a saree and a piece of material of the same coarse type, made in a jail workshop, for a blouse and petticoat. Quite how they were to make these without scissors, needles or thread was never explained, but we later heard that one of the wardresses had charged them each a part of their rice ration in return for making the garments on her machine.

One day not long before Christmas, the Chief Head Warder tested Kalpana's lock, found it dangerously loose and decided that it must be replaced. There was nowhere else to keep her, so we were allowed to share a cell at night once more. The Superintendent instructed that one other prisoner was to sleep with us to keep an eye on us; it was to be a different woman every night, to ensure that we had no chance to make any firm acquaintance or 'indoctrinate' anyone. This was a golden opportunity to find out more about our fellow prisoners' backgrounds and case histories. Very many of them came from communities designated in the Indian Constitution as Scheduled Castes and Scheduled Tribes and described as 'weaker sections' of the population. Chhotanagpur, the area in which Hazaribagh is situated, contains a large number of tribal people with their own languages, religion and culture. The Scheduled Castes are what Mahatma Gandhi called the Harijans, or People of God. Prior to that, they had been known by a name which describes what, in the eyes of many orthodox Hindus, they are still: the Untouchables.

Some of our nightly cell-mates had been arrested for brewing home-made liquor without a licence, some had become involved in disputes over land ownership, some were on murder or attempted murder charges. Very few of them ever got visits or letters from their families, often because these were too poor to raise the fare or to pay somebody to write the letter. As we listened to their often tragic stories, we became convinced that if our life in jail was to have any meaning at all we must devote our time and energy to helping our fellow prisoners in whatever way we could.

Sometimes during our walks, we noticed prisoners measuring rice into their aluminium tumblers or mustard oil into small cylindrical tobacco tins. Now one of the more confiding of our night-time companions told us that all the women secretly sold part of their rice, flour, oil, soap and molasses rations to members of the jail staff, who, in return, brought them either money or items they wanted from the market. The purchase price for prisoners' rations was far less than the current market rates, but nevertheless this unofficial arrangement allowed them to obtain some of the necessities not provided by the authorities, and little luxuries they felt the need of. Most of the women ate very little in order to save something to sell.

We decided that this sytem could also serve us. We carefully put aside a portion of our weekly rice ration; there were several things we wanted – toothpaste, rubber bands to tie back Kalpana's thick hair, and safety pins. The wardresses we approached were reluctant, afraid that we might spill the beans, but eventually we managed to come to an arrangement that enabled us to save up a few rupees. By Christmas we had enough to buy a small tin of Nescafé, a real luxury. For several weeks before the holiday we lived very frugally, to save enough flour and molasses to make some crude sweets, which we distributed to all the other women. On Christmas morning we had a marvellous surprise: somebody left a Christmas cake and a dozen bananas outside the gate for us. That day too, one of our sympathizers in the stores managed to slip a couple of pieces of liver into our holiday meat ration. We were better known outside the female ward than we had realized.

After Christmas, it grew colder still. We spent the nights huddled together wrapped in every item of clothing we possessed. One morning, the young Harijan prisoner who used to clean the latrines was shivering uncontrollably in his ragged vest and shorts. After asking the wardress's permission, Kalpana gave him one of our two shawls. As soon as he had finished his work and was about to return to the male sector, the wardress ran after him and instructed the duty warder to search him, accusing him of smuggling a letter for us. They found nothing. But the innocuous act of generosity had aroused the wardress's suspicion, and, more important, her jealousy. This emotion was understandable; probably she had never possessed a shawl as good as the one she had seen us give the sweeper. The outcome was unfortunate. That same day, the young sweeper was locked in solitary confinement, in fetters, and forbidden to come to the female ward again. We pleaded with the Chief Head Warder to withdraw this unwarranted punishment and explained the circumstances, but it was in vain. We were 'Naxalites', and instructions were that we were not to have contact with other prisoners.

Shortly after this, the Superintendent came one day to tell me that permission had been granted by the Bihar Government for me to meet members of Amalendu's family. They had, it seemed, got half-way to 'recognizing' our marriage. Amalendu's father would be visiting me at the beginning of February. Unfortunately, some days afterwards a letter which Amalendu had secretly written to me was discovered by an unsympathetic warder, who reported the incident to the Jailer. Amalendu was put in iron bar fetters as a punishment, and visiting permission for both of us was cancelled until further notice. Tears came to my eyes when I thought of him in the dreaded *dandaberi*, an iron ring round either ankle, each attached to a twenty-inch iron rod which in turn joined up with a third rod reaching up to the waist, where the whole contraption was hooked into the prisoner's waistband or on to a piece of cord. The fetters were heavy and a severe restriction to movement of any kind: it was impossible for anyone wearing them to walk, sit, sleep, bathe or use the lavatory in the normal manner.

These incidents reminded us that, despite any seeming relaxation on the part of the authorities, our existence was extremely precarious.

One of the most important institutions of jail life was fasting. Every Sunday, all those prisoners who wanted to were allowed to fast, and to order some little luxury instead of their normal food ration: *bidi* (cigarettes made of rolled leaves), *khoini* (a kind of snuff), and sometimes sugar or other items of food, if available. This arrangement, at first sight humane and lenient, was in fact of great service to the authorities in keeping the prisoners as submissive as possible. By granting such privileges, they kept the prisoners in constant fear of having them taken away and thus prevented them from speaking out on other matters. For all those people connected with the stores, fasting was a source of profit; the prisoners were always given items less in value than the day's food they had to forfeit. The women were quite aware of this exploitation but chose to keep quiet rather than lose the opportunity of fasting altogether. The few coins they got from members of the staff in exchange for their sugar or *bidi* were a welcome addition to their savings and enabled them to buy medicines and cosmetics, clothing, bangles or seasonal vegetables from the market. All the week they carefully saved a little rice or flour from each day's ration for their Sunday meal. Early on Sunday morning women and children could be seen scouring the vegetable garden for edible leaves to accompany their boiled rice or *lopsi* (a porridge of flour and salt). The actual vegetables were consumed by the matine and staff but they usually let the prisoners have the potato, radish and mustard leaves that they did not want themselves. In the absence of adequate facilities, cooking on Sundays was a problem; everyone felt hungry, and there were only two fires, the matine's and ours. She only allowed her favourites to cook on hers, and then not until her own elaborate meal was ready. Some of the women cooked on improvised fires lit with the sticks they had been given for cleaning their teeth each morning. Our small coal fire, lit in an oil tin caked with dried mud, was in demand all day long, and inevitably some of us went hungry waiting for others' food to be cooked.

Another Sunday event was *mulakati* (meetings). Once every few weeks the women with male relatives in the jail were allowed to meet them for a few minutes' conversation in the jail office, under the supervision of an Assistant Jailer. A surprisingly large number of them had fathers, brothers, sons or husbands in prison, usually held on the same charges as themselves. Most of them saved something from their rations to cook for their menfolk on *mulakati* days. They would soak some rice or a few chick peas in water overnight; in the morning, these would be ground with a stone to a paste, which, mixed with a paltry amount of molasses or salt, was fashioned into flat cakes and cooked in a little of the mustard oil they were given for lubricating their bodies.

At about three o'clock those who were going to meet their relatives smoothed the sarees they had washed and dried that morning, combed their hair and tied their offerings in pieces of clean rag or newspaper. Some time before five o'clock the bell would ring and the duty warder would open the gate to allow them out on to the gravel track that led to the office, checking each name against a list as they went out. Fifteen minutes later they would return with all the latest gossip. Male prisoners, apart from Naxalites, had limited freedom to move about in their own part of the jail, and were able to relay many titbits of information they had gleaned. There were rumours of trials, transfers, visits of high officials, somebody's release, another's bail. Kalpana and I used to await the return from *mulakati* with considerable enthusiasm, in the anticipation of hearing something interesting.

At first I had been puzzled by the way people addressed each other, but, after a time, it seemed natural to call women older than I *ma* (mother) or *mousi* (auntie), as the Indian people do; it was considered disrespectful to address persons senior to oneself by name. To most of the other women I was either *beti* (daughter), or *didi* (elder sister). One however insisted on calling me *nani* (granny), though she was old enough to be my mother. When reprimanded by one of the other women she retorted, 'Well, she must be older than I am, her hair is completely white.' It was not the only time that my blonde hair was taken as a sign of old age. Police officers, warders and other officials too, always estimated me to be much older than my twenty-seven years.

One of those whom we called *ma*, was Saibunissa, a Muslim woman of about forty-five. She, her husband, her three young sons and a nephew had all been jailed for twenty years after a dispute over land inheritance that had led to a fight in which her brother-in-law had died. When they were sentenced her youngest son was about thirteen years old and had already spent five years in jail. Even the oldest was only about nineteen when we first saw him. Her three youngest children were outside. Often she cried, wondering how three girls left at the the age of three, four and six years could fend for themselves in the raw reality of village society, where, if they fell into the wrong hands, they might be used as servants, or worse still, sold as slaves, and, later, maybe, prostitutes.

Because she had been separated from her own children, Saibunissa really felt for us, and treated us with great affection. We would hover round the fire as she squatted making pancakes of wheat flour and water on the iron griddle. She smiled as we reached out for each pancake as it came hot from the fire and devoured it with obvious relish, happy to think that we enjoyed her cooking. Most of the prisoners were surprised to discover that we had no objections to eating food they cooked; they were used to being treated as 'unclean' or 'untouchable'. When they realized that we really appreciated what they made, they overwhelmed us with gifts of food from their own portions. I was moved by the generosity and open-heartedness of women who had so little but so unhesitatingly shared whatever they possessed.

Another of our special friends was Rohini, a young peasant woman who was also on a murder charge. She had enormous strength and capacity for work and never tired of digging the garden, washing the wardress's clothes and helping the matine with her domestic tasks. She was always pressing us to let her do our work too. She wanted to wash our clothes, clean our cell, even massage us, but we explained that being literate did not mean that we should scorn manual work. Unused to seeing somebody even a little educated or prosperous do his own work, our fellow prisoners felt it as a reflection upon themselves when we broke coal for the fire, swept our cell or scoured our cooking utensils. But once the initial doubt was overcome our willingness to work brought us closer to them.

Rohini told us of her secret wish to learn to read and write. After that, in the afternoons when work was done, Kalpana used to spend a couple of hours teaching her the Hindi alphabet. This later had an adverse effect that we did not anticipate.

# 4. The Shooting

Sunday, 25 April 1971. There was fasting as usual, and it was also *mulakati* day. By this time, both Kalpana and I had tried our hands at village cooking, and from morning I had been squatting on a folded blanket in front of the fire cooking countless chick pea fritters for the women to take to their male relatives. The stone floor around the fire was splashed with oil and ashes, my hands were covered in dried chick pea paste, my saree was smeared with the remnants of molasses and oil. Suddenly, the matine came running: '*Didi*, you have to go to the office. Your *mulakati* has come.' At first I did not believe her; it was not the first time we had played tricks of that kind on each other. Not until the Chief Head Warder himself came to fetch me did I realize that she was telling the truth and that, after nearly eleven months in jail, I was going to have a visitor who was not a consular official. I hastily combed my hair, uneven and scruffy after so long without a haircut. I had no other saree to put on so wore the oil-splashed one I had been cooking in since morning which had been given me by Kalpana's mother. My original slacks and T-shirt had long since disintegrated and I had grown accustomed to wearing Indian clothes.

In the office, littered with files and papers and crowded with clerks and convict writers, Amalendu's aged parents were seated, an island of calm and dignity in a sea of confusion. They beckoned to me to sit down. I shocked the onlookers by not bending to touch their feet, as a dutiful daughter-in-law should. They had already seen Amalendu and his brother but had not been allowed to meet us all together. I was touched by their effort in making the 500-mile round trip to visit us. They had brought clothes, home-made coconut sweets, perfumed soap, a palm-leaf fan to cool me in the summer's heat. I tried to allay their obvious anxiety about my well-being, and was permitted to talk with them for ten minutes before returning to the female ward.

All the rest of the day I paced the cell and compound, angry with myself for being caught off guard so that I had forgotten to tell them all the things I had been preparing for months. I felt at once happy to have seen them and guilty at having put them to so much trouble and expense. I was upset at not having seen Amalendu. Visits were always an unsettling experience, making one remember life outside, people one loved, things one was missing. It invariably took me two days to get back to 'normal' afterwards.

The coconut sweets posed a problem: Kalpana and I wanted to share them with everyone, yet still have enough for ourselves. In this our behaviour contrasted with that of most of the other women, who, if they were ever given anything, however small, immediately shared it out, as if they wanted everyone to benefit from their good fortune. In the end we overcame our greed and shared our sweets, being particularly careful to be absolutely fair; in the general situation of hardship, even a trifling inequality could arouse envy that rankled until one day it burst out in a battle of insult and accusation.

It was the petty envy of women living together in unnatural and difficult circumstances that eventually put an abrupt end to these months of comparative relaxation in our conditions. Kalpana's lessons with Rohini had aroused the jealousy of the matine, who considered that she should be given preference in all matters and saw in Rohini's new-found literacy a possible challenge to her own position. At night, when we were locked up separately and could not overhear her, she used to taunt Rohini, who several times came to us upset and weeping, unable to ignore the petty insults. One day, exasperated by the matine's pettiness, we warned her to leave Rohini alone. This was a serious mistake on our part. She started planning her revenge.

Some days later, she reported to the Chief Head Warder that she had seen Kalpana hiding something at the end of the garden.

This report happened to coincide with a general tightening of security, following a warning from the Special Branch police that Naxalite prisoners were likely to make an escape bid. Only the day before an order had come that three prisoners were to sleep with us at night, instead of one. Under the circumstances, the Warder had no option but to report what the matine had told him to his superior the Jailer. Sense of duty prevented him from telling us, but the seriousness of his expression as he locked us in that evening was warning enough; we had spent one whole year in prison and had developed a high sensitivity to the slightest variation in the mood of our keepers. That day we were certain that something was afoot.

After the Warder had departed, one of the wardresses, on pretext of checking our lock, came and called to us softly. She warned us that the Superintendent and Jailer were coming to search us and told us to give her anything that needed hiding. We gave her the few rupees we had saved and a couple of smuggled letters we had kept. Then we and our companions settled down as if we knew nothing, taking off our sarees as we always did on the hot summer nights and lying on the bare stone floor in our underclothes. At ten o'clock there was a sudden flashing of lights along the stone wall and the sound of men's voices. The officers had arrived without a word or sound of warning, ignoring the bell they were supposed to ring on entering the female ward, so as to surprise us completely. They came straight to our cell, and, not even waiting for us to get dressed, flashed powerful torches on us and ordered us outside. They locked Kalpana and me in the adjoining empty cell while they ransacked our belongings. Twenty minutes later, the three steps leading up to the cell were strewn with letters, bottles of oil, soap, cotton wool, clothes, books and newspapers. Determined not to be intimidated, the two of us sang at the tops of our voices, accompanying our songs with drumbeats on an aluminium plate we found in the cell. Afterwards, a wardress told us that the Superintendent had been quite unnerved by our singing. Once our possessions had been thoroughly gone over, a wardress was sent to search our persons. She found nothing more than a lead pencil Kalpana had hidden in the waistband of her petticoat. After tipping out our entire coal ration on the floor, they departed. We tried to settle down, but were quite unable to rest after the shock of the night's event.

The purge was not over. In the morning our cell was not unlocked in the usual way: we had to remain confined in our cage while about twenty convicts, accompanied by several warders, swarmed across our compound, uprooted bushes, chopped down trees and dug up the whole expanse of garden. When their rampage was over, our beloved margosa tree had been reduced to a twelve-foot totem pole, all the jasmine bushes were gone, as were the bougainvillaea, guava, mango and lemon trees and the sweet-smelling gulaichi flowers. When we were finally let out, we walked despondently around the scarred expanse of bare red earth, as if mourning the loss of friends. The contact with Nature that the trees and garden had brought us had contributed greatly to making imprisonment bearable. Now it had been taken away.

After this episode, the jail seemed transformed overnight into a fortress. The weeks that followed were filled with an intangible foreboding. The wardresses, shocked and scared out of their previous indulgence towards us, warned the other prisoners not to come near us and threatened to beat them if they told us what they heard of goings-on inside and outside the prison. We found ourselves isolated, angry and helpless, surrounded by a sea of suspicion bordering on hostility. We spent the days restlessly, unable to concentrate on anything, always wondering what was happening beyond our walls. We heard rumours that all Naxalite prisoners had been searched. I kept wondering about Amalendu. In solitary confinement still, he must have known even less than we about what was going on. I knew he would be worrying about me, but there was no way of letting him know that I was all right. The warders had stepped up their vigilance and there was little hope of sending a message.

Once more, we were separated and locked alone in our cells at night. Our newspapers, books, letters and food were checked and scrutinized by the wardresses and matine. There was scarcely a trace of the former friendliness and sympathy. The barrenness of the devastated garden was reflected in our own mentality. Unable to sing, joke or plan variations to our menu, we were subdued, tense and insecure, wondering what would come next. The Warder's evening inspections were more penetrating than ever. One day he took away the bottles of mustard and coconut oil we had for cooking and for Kalpana's long hair. All my protests had no effect on him. Bottles were not allowed, he must show them to the Jailer. The whole thing was ridiculous; the bottles had been there long before the search, he had simply not noticed them. Now he accused me of breaking the rules, as if I had deliberately disobeyed instructions. And, furious as I felt, there was nothing I could do.

Luckily, we had not lost all our friends. One who remembered us was Sukri, a Harijan woman who worked as a lavatory cleaner in a factory not far from Hazaribagh. She and her husband had been charged with receiving stolen copper wire. Normally there would not have been much expense or difficulty involved in getting bail in this relatively minor case; but, because of their lack of land or property and the dishonesty of their lawyer, they had spent all their savings and were still in jail. We had realized after the first few weeks that the lawyer was swindling them and had urged her to tell her husband not to give him any more money, but in their anxiety to get back to work before their jobs were lost, they had naïvely carried on paying him till their resources were exhausted.

Now, in our time of difficulty, Sukri remembered our advice and stood by us. Every fortnight she used to see her husband in court. He had been working as a sweeper in one of the Naxalite wards, and like the male Naxalites themselves and all those prisoners considered sympathetic to them, had been put in fetters and confined all day to his cell. Whenever she returned from court, as soon as she found the opportunity to have a few quiet words with us, Sukri used to tell us what had been happening to the other Naxalite prisoners. The searches in the male section had been far more thorough than ours, and were repeated night after night. It was said that some sticks of dynamite had been found planted in the wall of one of the wards. There were rumours that the convict who had smuggled them in had some-how been betrayed to the Special Branch police, and that the Superintendent had been summoned late at night from his club to supervise a search. We asked other people about these ru-mours, but they were never confirmed by any other source.

One day, Sukri came back from court with a smuggled letter from some of our co-defendants. It warned us to be vigilant and not to allow ourselves to be provoked in any way. A sympathetic warder had told them that there was a plan for a general assault on the Naxalite wards next time the monthly practice alarm bell was sounded. He had heard it being discussed in the jail office. This letter alarmed us more than ever, but we were not sure what to do to prepare ourselves.

The jail staff themselves were suffering from the increased security measures. Every time they came on duty or left for home they had to undergo a search, so were unable to smuggle out the food and other items they had been in the habit of taking from the stores or buying from prisoners. We were told that some of the younger warders, whose wages were very low and who depended entirely on the cheap supplies they obtained from inside the jail, had devised an ingenious, if risky way of getting round the new restrictions. Those on duty in the watchtowers used to lower a bucket on a rope into the inner jail compound, to be filled by the prisoners below. This would then be hauled up, complete with rice, potatoes, flour, lentils or mustard oil, and lowered down the outside wall to the warders' waiting colleagues or families. If caught, they would, of course, have lost their jobs.

In general, the jail staff were annoyed by the new regulations and constant checks and searches, and felt resentful towards the Naxalites, whose presence, they thought, was causing them all this trouble. In our ward too, the matine and one of the ward-resses often reminded the other prisoners that jail had been 'like home' before the Naxalites came and spoiled it all. However, the women had deeply resented the Superintendent's action in uprooting the fruit trees and vegetable garden. Being agricultural workers, and having had a hard struggle to grow sufficient food, they regarded the destruction of anything that would provide food as a sin, and prophesied that he would receive due punishment from *bhagwan* (god). Though fear of reprisals kept them away from us for a few weeks, they gradually started coming to chat again.

After the search, the Superintendent resumed his frequent visits. Even at night he kept constant vigil, carrying out rounds of the watchtowers and duty posts to check that none of the warders was sleeping. Three young warders caught asleep on duty were suspended. All night we could hear totals being shouted from one tower to another, bars in the adjoining wards being tested with an iron rod, padlocks being rattled and bells being rung. In the daytime too, the Superintendent roamed the jail, looking for anything suspicious. Entering our ward one afternoon, he sent the duty wardress on ahead to check our cell, telling her that we had hidden a pistol to shoot him. Another day, lifting up the sacks that covered our food rations, he saw two lemons the doctor had prescribed for me, and, prodding them with his stick, demanded to know who had brought us guavas. Not until he had smelled them was he satisfied.

That year it rained almost every day from April till October. Our clothes and books were damp and covered with mould spots, flour and rice were bitter to the taste. The rain seeped through walls and ceiling into coal and firewood, blankets and sacks. Outside, large areas of Bihar were under water for weeks on end; crops were ruined. Our daily vegetable was blackened potatoes that left a nasty stinging sensation in the mouth. Skies were permanently overcast, the garden nothing but a swamp.

One Sunday afternoon, in a torrential downpour, I was trying to urge some life into the fire to make our evening *chapatis*, when the alarm bell started clanging, followed by the urgent blowing of warders' whistles. The wardress on duty ran to lock us all in our cells. Almost before our padlocks were fastened, the shooting started. For the next two hours I listened, trapped in the cell, helplessly clutching the bars, while shots rang out from every corner of the jail. The wardress herself took shelter for fear of being hit by flying bullets. My heart was pounding, my whole body trembling. The agony of not knowing what was happening filled my head till it felt as if it would burst. At about five o'clock the Chief Head Warder appeared, beretless, hair tousled, barefoot and bedraggled, to check the total of female prisoners. At nine o'clock a group of Bihar Military Police from the camps that surrounded the jail came to search us. Their officer sneered as he informed me that some Naxalites had been killed. Our cells were not opened again until late next morning. That day we questioned the wardresses about what had happened but they had been bound to silence by the threats of the Chief Head Warder. One of them, seeing how upset we were, tried to soothe us by telling us that there had been a tussle between some warders and prisoners over tobacco and *bidi*, and that the shots we had heard had been fired into the air. We knew it was not true.

The next morning, one of the convicts who came every day with the women's food motioned to us by passing his hand across his throat and raising his fingers that ten prisoners had been killed. I kept wondering whether Amalendu was among them. Sometimes I imagined him dead, at others I tried to convince myself that he was all right. It was several weeks before I was sure that he was alive and unhurt, when his sisters came to visit us and assured me that they had seen and spoken to him. In fact none of my co-defendants had been involved in the incident. The shooting took place on 25 July 1971, and it was late August when I read in a copy of the London *Times* which the Deputy High Commission had recently started sending, and which the jail authorities had not thought to censor, that sixteen Naxalites were killed that day. It was later still when I discovered that the *Times of India* had reported that twelve of them had been beaten to death, and months afterwards that a wardress told me the full story of what had happened. Apparently, a group of Naxalites had broken out of their cells and gone to the jail gate, intending to escape. The Jailer had seen them and had given the order for warders to shoot. After shooting down the men involved in the actual break attempt, armed warders, aided by 'trusty' convicts, had gone on a rampage of the other Naxalite wards, dragging prisoners out of their cells, beating them, and shooting some at point blank range. What had started as an incident involving a small number of prisoners developed into indiscriminate killing. Apart from the sixteen killed, a month later thirty-one were still in the jail hospital with wounds and injuries. And though, several years afterwards, the Chief Head Warder told me that, had he been on duty at the time he could have prevented any bloodshed, it seemed that the break attempt by a small group of Naxalites had given the authorities the opportunity they were looking for.

That year forty-five youths had been killed already in shooting incidents in jails at Midnapur, Berhampur, Dum Dum, Patna, and Calcutta. Many more were killed later. There was an inquiry into the Hazaribagh incident, but, not surprisingly, the investigator, a retired judge, found the shooting to have been justified. The 'trusty' convicts who had helped beat some men to death were each rewarded with five years' remission.

As if events inside jail were not enough, one day a slip in censorship revealed that the bodies of eleven youths, suspected Naxalites, had been found scattered alongside the road in Barasat, North Calcutta. There was speculation that the police were responsible for these murders and for similar and mysterious large-scale killings in the Dum Dum and Diamond Harbour suburbs of Calcutta. Several times, the press reported that Naxalite youths had been beaten to death in police stations. A reader wrote to one of the papers that he was unable to sleep at night because of the screams of people being tortured in the police station near his home. Kalpana had not heard from her family for some time; afterwards we came to know that one of her brothers and a nephew had been arrested for alleged Naxalite sympathies. They were held three months before being released.

A lady, the relative of a jail official whom I met by chance at a much later stage in my imprisonment, told me that in those dark days, in villages near her home in Birbhum District, West Bengal, youths had been called out of their homes by police and shot on the doorstep. It seemed that the law enforcement agencies had turned to wholesale terror in order to turn the population away from the Naxalite path.

After that July Sunday, the jail took on a new appearance. At the time of its building, Hazaribagh, with its trees and gardens, had been considered a model jail. Now, dozens of mango, guava, jackfruit and woodapple trees were chopped down in order to give the guards in the watchtowers a clear view into all the wards. Days were filled with the sound of trees being hacked and felled. As they toppled, one by one, it seemed that the barriers that had protected us were falling, that now there was nothing but an open battlefield between us and our keepers. When they had cut down the two big mango trees that lay just beyond our walls, we could clearly see the guard in the nearest watchtower, about sixty yards away, standing all day in rain and wind, rifle at the ready. It seemed as if they were clearing the

Hazaribagh – Watchtower

paths for another shooting. Even as we lay in our cells at night, we felt vulnerable, being in full view of the watchtower and in range of the guard's bullets.

I felt like a prisoner of war, yet how could I convey what was happening to anyone outside? Knowing that my parents would be alarmed at the lack of news from me, particularly as the shooting incident had been reported in the British press, I tried to write a few lines as if all was well and my life peaceful and pleasant. No doubt the censors were pleased with me. I hated writing half-truths, but I knew that was the only way any news of me at all would reach my family.

Prisoners went about their daily work subdued and frightened, warders searched everyone entering our ward and looked at us suspiciously. Some of them took to warning the other women to keep quiet about poor conditions and injustices or run the risk of being classified as Naxalites and locked in solitary confinement. Yet amidst all this, Saibunissa's husband, already grey and wizened, took the risk of going to the cell block where Amalendu was kept to try and find out how he was. Though in fact he was not even able to enter the top security block, the same day the old man was accused of aiding Naxalites and locked in a cell, where he remained until one of his sons paid the Chief Head Warder ten rupees to unlock him. I felt conscious-stricken to have been the cause of his suffering, but he thought nothing of it. He sent me a message assuring me that he would try again.

All through that terrible monsoon season there was a press build-up towards war with Pakistan. Newspaper articles were crude attempts to arouse national feeling. East Pakistan had been in a state of civil war since March, refugees were crossing the border into India and living in appalling conditions in camps around Calcutta. It seemed as if India was paving the way for intervention. In August, the Indio-Soviet Treaty of Peace, Friendship and Co-operation was signed, and widely interpreted as a significant step towards emboldening the Indian Government to send troops into East Bengal.

Towards the end of August 1971, we had yet another surprise visit from the Superintendent, this time accompanied by a police officer who refused to identify himself or tell us where he was from. He started questioning me as to my name, nationality and passport number, all details long in the possession of the authorities. Kalpana whispered to me that there was no point in going through the whole thing yet again. Her casual remark was met by an unexpected and violent reaction from the Superintendent. Raising his stick, he ordered her into the next-door cell. When I attempted to follow, he barred my way and barked to me to stay right where I was and answer the policeman's questions. I had already been in prison fifteen months, and had been told that there was a rule forbidding police department officials from entering the jail premises; I decided that I would on no account answer any more questions.

I sat down, silent, and refused either to answer or to sign any statement. The Superintendent was meanwhile having a tussle with Kalpana, pushing her into the next cell and locking her up for having been impudent enough to open her mouth. He then came back to me and told me that I 'must' speak. I remained silent. In the end he instructed that all my books and papers be taken away. I would in future have no reading material and would be locked up, as at the beginning, day and night. I informed him that in that case I would go on indefinite hunger strike, seeing that I had committed no infringement of the jail rules and had every right not to answer questions. Saying, 'All right, if you can't open your mouth to talk you can't open it to eat either,' he departed.

That night we were allowed no water, no oil lamp. Yet, miraculously, next morning our cells were opened. We decided, however, not to abandon our hunger strike, until our newspapers and books were restored to us. We were puzzled at the unusual liberality exercised in unlocking us. By afternoon, our books and papers had been returned and nothing more had been said.

Next morning we understood why the authorities had not wanted to intensify the situation. Before daylight, the bell outside our gate rang loudly and, a minute afterwards, a wardress was outside Kalpana's cell telling her to get ready for transfer to Calcutta. The next hour was spent in hasty preparation. We had to divide all the possessions we had shared into two. As I plaited Kalpana's thick shiny hair for the last time we reminded each other of the measures we had discussed for keeping in touch. It occurred to me that Amalendu might be transferred too, and I gave her a message for him in case she happened to see him. In fact he was taken to Calcutta that day but I did not know for sure until two months later.

Soon after the other prisoners had been unlocked, Kalpana was called away. All along we had known that we should be parted sooner or later, and yet, when the parting came, it was unexpected. As I walked back to my cell after saying goodbye at the gate of our ward, I fought back the tears; I did not want the other women, who were very soft-hearted, to be upset by seeing me cry.

Saibunissa and Rohini came to sit with me, comforting and consoling me and assuring me that they would take care of me. Saibunissa made me some pancakes and brought a little sugar she had hoarded to sprinkle on them, knowing my fondness for sweets. I was touched, but still I knew that I would miss Kalpana more deeply than I could convey to them. During the time spent together, we had grown very close. The daughter of a well-to-do middle-class family, her feeling for the sufferings of her fellow-countrymen had led her to reject the easy path of a 'good' arranged marriage, comfortable home and children, to go and work in the Calcutta slums. Contact with hunger, disease, violence and death had toughened her; I, in comparison, had led a soft and sheltered life and now that she was no longer there, I felt vulnerable. Yet, despite this tough exterior, I had seen her cry as she listened to the tragic life history of a fellow-prisoner, and forget to eat, drink or comb her hair as she concentrated on nursing a sick woman. I missed her ability to laugh at difficulties, to mock at those who tried to break our spirits, her readiness to act against injustice and her selflessness in helping those in need. In the years that followed, many a time I wished that she was there to add strength to all my struggles with the authorities.

That evening I held Prokash, a little boy whom Kalpana liked very much, in my arms as I walked around the garden, wondering where Kalpana and Amalendu were and what would happen when they were taken to Lalbazaar, the notorious Calcutta police headquarters. Pointing beyond the central watchtower, Prokash said, 'Kalpana *mousi* is there. When is she coming back?' I wished I could have answered his question.

# 5. Companions

Now that the cell next to mine was empty, night times were lonely. After a week or two, Leoni, a young wardress, who had been feeling sorry for me, started coming to sit with me. She was hardly out of her teens, and I wondered how she had come to be a prison wardress. She told me that after the death of her stepfather, his sons by his first marriage had thrown her mother and five young children out of the house, fearing that they would lay claim to part of the dead man's land. Leoni remembered keenly the poverty they had experienced. Having no home, mother and children slept in the courtyard of a family of their acquaintance; they had no plates or utensils and ate their once-daily meal of boiled rice from big leaves. The only variety in their diet was provided by the boiled leaves of a tree that stood in the yard. Eventually, she and her mother found casual jobs as building labourers, carting loads of bricks and cement in trays on their heads. Now she considered herself fortunate to have landed a government job that guaranteed her some security, regular food, and sufficient money to help pay for the schooling of her younger brothers.

Like several of the other wardresses in the jail, she came from a family of tribal people who had been converted by Christian missionaries, but, unlike some of the others, she did not regard the unconverted members of her tribe as *jonglis*, or barbarians, and did not try to imitate European manners. As I got to know her better, I developed a genuine respect for her courage and straightforwardness and came to look upon her as a friend. One marked difference between her and other members of the jail staff was that she never accused the prisoners of being criminals or told them that they should count themselves lucky that the government fed them. She knew that one did not necessarily have to be criminal to get into jail. Remembering the days when she had nothing, she used to save her old clothes and bring them for those prisoners who were most in need, and in general was very kind and helpful to all of us.

That year, on Durga Puja, the biggest of the Hindu festivals, I was allowed the 'treat' of accompanying the other women, after the male prisoners had been locked up, to the building somewhat inaccurately called the 'School and Library', that housed an image of the goddess Durga made by prisoners. The building was nothing but a smaller version of the women's dormitory and was used as a cell for male prisoners. There was no sign of a book or any equipment that might have justified its name. Hollow-eyed men squatted inside like silent ghosts on their folded blankets. We crowded outside the locked and barred door to gaze at 'Mother Durga'. Behind us stood some of the office staff, all decked out in their holiday best, to supervise us. All at once the awed silence was broken by Prokash's crippled mother: 'Durga ma, my boy's testicles have swollen, please help me.' There was a snigger from the clerks and a suppressed giggle from us. Then an Assistant Jailer said: 'Who's that? Bisni? I might have known!' True enough, Prokash had been suffering from a swelling of the testicles, and his mother had decided that, as the doctor had not been able to cure him and the charm she had bought from the market had not worked, she would appeal to the goddess herself. Curiously enough he did recover soon afterwards. Whenever we laughed at the recollection of her prayer to the goddess, she had a ready answer: 'Well, it worked, didn't it?'

Shortly after the holiday there was an alteration in supervision arrangements. A new wardress was appointed; henceforth there would be two on day duty and three at night. At the same time searchlights were installed on all the watchtowers, though those on the one nearest to me did not actually work until over a year later. And I was given company at night. Three prisoners were ordered to share my cell, not out of consideration for my loneliness but in order to watch me and report on my activities. These changes were a direct result of the 25 July shooting.

On the face of it, we were a strange foursome, but in November Hazaribagh nights started to be chilly and the earth, still damp from the monsoon rains, sent early morning mists through our bars; we made up our beds close to each other for warmth and spent the increasingly long evenings telling stories and posing riddles to each other. I was not a very active participant in this as I still couldn't speak the local version of Hindi very well, but, now that there was no Kalpana to speak English to, my knowledge of the language was rapidly increasing.

Nearest to the bars slept Bulkani, old, skinny and asthmatic, a retired colliery worker, in prison without trial for three years already on a petty theft charge. She was always feverish and did not feel the cold, so was quite happy to form a barrier between us and the night air. Next to her lay Mohini, arrested with her husband and eldest son after a fight over land in which her sister-in-law had died. She had left four young children at home and often wondered how they would manage their small farm. Whenever, on festivals and holidays, we were given something 'special' in the way of food, she would sit crying, unable to eat, thinking of her children. Occasionally one son used to visit her. After each visit she cried for hours on end, on hearing how they were getting deeper into debt. Once he came to tell her that their two oxen had died, and as they had no means of ploughing their land, he was thinking of mortgaging it to take her bail.

Next to me slept Panno, an elderly widow from the Santhal tribe, famous for its militancy and in particular for its armed revolt against the British in the eighteen-fifties. At night she would jerk and mumble and whimper in her sleep, seeing nightmares of the daughter whom she had killed by hitting her over the head with a big stone. Sometimes in the morning she would say to me: 'I had to do it. The bitch brought shame on me. I had to do it.' Her daughter had become pregnant by the son of their village headman, who then refused to consider marrying her. Ashamed and embarrassed by the taunts and abuse of the other villagers, Panno had at first given the girl a thrashing. Even that punishment, however, was not enough to mitigate the disgrace she had brought upon her family, and one day Panno had taken her into the jungle to collect firewood, then attacked her from behind. The old woman had immediately surrendered to the police, and, after four years in jail, had been sentenced to twenty years' imprisonment.

Looking at Panno, I could not conceive of her in a state of fury. Diligent and quiet to the point of meekness, she cried if ever anyone addressed harsh words to her, and was quite unable to answer back. Sometimes she came to me with a few coins to count how much money she had saved from her fasting, or to check any amount a wardress had given her. On Sundays she often gave me some flour and a lump of molasses she had saved and said, 'Daughter, make me some *pitha*' (a kind of sweet dumpling).

Hers was the first of several cases I came across in which murder had been committed either to avenge or to protect the family honour. There was no thought of evading the law. Those who killed in this way knew that they would have to spend years in prison, but accepted it as a fair price for having performed their duty. On the whole the village people considered the laws and conduct which the state tried to impose on them as irrelevant. In all my five years in prison I hardly ever came across any other type of premeditated murder.

Because of the restricted lives they had led, in which each person's village was a 'country', whose borders marked the limit of her experience, my fellow prisoners lived in a world of ghosts, witches and evil spirits, kings, queens and superstitions. Most had never seen a newspaper before, and crowded round each day to find out what was written in mine. Sometimes, hearing that significant events were described there, one of them would ask if there was any news of her case or her village. Though they knew the word 'government', nobody had ever told them how the country was run. However, they were eager to learn, and also asked me many other questions: where kerosene oil came from, how paper was made, how the newspaper was printed, and so on.

Even when I knew the answers, it was very difficult to explain in my limited Hindi, but I did my best.

When the cauliflowers in the garden were attacked by cater-pillars, Mohini said it was because someone had entered the garden during menstruation. If anyone was repeatedly ill, it was put down to the evil eye. Some put black marks on their chil-dren's foreheads and tied charms around their waists to ward off evil spirits. Once there was a vehement argument over an old prisoner who was subject to fits in which her eyes would roll and she shook all over. Some of the women said she was a witch and would eat their children; every night there were quarrels over who was to sleep nearest to her. I persuaded the warder to let her sleep in our cell for a few nights to prove that she was harmless. After that, peace was restored.

As we sat patching our torn clothes or turning the grindstone to make flour from roast chick peas, I would listen to tales of village life, which were a source of endless fascination. Nearly all the women belonged to the poorer sections of the peasantry and lived in homes their families had built themselves from mud, wood and thatch. Though child marriages are banned by law in India, they had almost without exception been married in early childhood to husbands 'negotiated' for them by third parties on behalf of their parents, and had been sent to their father-in-law's house after their first menstruation. They had seen their husbands for the first time on the wedding day itself. Some of those who lived near towns or had been to the cinema knew about the European style of marriage, which they called 'love marriage', using the English phrase; but they regarded it as something reserved for film stars and the very rich, those who could afford to break with tradition without incurring society's disapproval. They told alarming tales of girls who had run off with men of their own choice and had been forced to drink ram's blood, paraded on a donkey before the whole village, made to live in a hut away from other people, or had their hair shaved off to atone for their 'crime'. If a woman was in disgrace, her family would have to pay a fine to the village council and stand the whole village a feast in order to buy back their caste and avoid ostracism. This was known literally as *jatbhat*, caste rice.

The husband was such a revered figure that most of them would not even utter his name, much to the frustration of clerks on official business, who sometimes could not find out a woman's husband's name to fill in their forms, because she refused to say it. Sometimes she could be induced to whisper the hallowed sounds into the ear of an older woman, who was at liberty to relay it to the clerk. Other 'sins' were to have one's head uncovered in the presence of male persons, or to talk to one's father-in-law or one's husband's elder brother.

Many of my companions had been regularly beaten by their husbands, and, though resentful, thought it the natural order of things. One of the women told me that her husband hit her for putting too much salt in his food, another because his rice was cold. None of them, however hungry they might be, could eat until after the men of the house had eaten. One woman was not allowed into the house at all during the days of her monthly period. The more prosperous among them had been confined almost entirely to the house and its surroundings, though the poorer, who had to work for their living, had led slightly less restricted lives, working in the fields or sometimes on building sites. Quite a lot of them had a co-wife, in some cases the widow of their husband's elder brother.

Now that there was nobody at all who knew anything about the Western way of life, I found myself quite unconsciously adapting to my companions' code of morality. I was very careful not to talk loudly or laugh in front of the warders or male prisoners, so as not to be thought 'shameless'. I found myself avoiding the garden during menstruation, so that nobody could blame me if the vegetables were attacked by pests. I succumbed to their exhortations to put vermilion in the parting of my hair, so as to make it clear that I was not looking for another husband.

At the beginning of December, the inevitable war with Pakistan started. Planes flew overhead; women and children ran out each time to watch them and exclaim. Workmen came to hang tin cans over the light bulbs that illuminated the compound. At night I could hear heavy lorries. Seventeen days later, India had won the war, and the jingoistic newspaper articles changed to exultations over the defeat of the 'enemy'. Indian troops remained in East Bengal, and Pakistani prisoners of war were held in India for over two years.

Several days after the start of the war, Rohini, Saibunissa and Panno were transferred to Bhagalpur, the only jail in Bihar designed specially for women convicts. Another woman who had recently been sentenced to five years' imprisonment was to have gone too, but she had an acquaintance among the male prisoners who gave an Assistant Jailer sixty-five rupees to allow her to stay in Hazaribagh, which was nearer to her home. Another reason for staying was that she was in the process of arranging the marriage of her six-year-old daughter to the son of one of the convicts of her caste.

After Rohini's departure, I heard that in the office she had asked for the return of the silver bracelets and necklace she had been told to deposit there on entry into the jail. They could not be found, and she was sent off with the assurance that they 'would be forwarded'. This was the first of several cases I heard of where prisoners pleaded in vain with the jail staff for the return of their money and valuables.

On the same weekend as Rohini left, I quite unexpectedly received a postcard from Amalendu, who was in Alipur Central Jail, Calcutta. I had not bothered to write to him, assuming that my letter would never reach him. The clerk who brought his postcard, the same one who had taken me for a man when I first arrived and who had developed a soft spot for me, was almost as delighted as I was. Amalendu's father had written to say that conditions in Calcutta jails were much worse than ours, and I had been concerned about him. His few lines temporarily relieved my anxiety, and, prosaic as they were, meant as much as any love letter. During the next three and a half years I received three more postcards from him, out of the many he wrote.

The departure of Rohini and Saibunissa reminded me once more of the transitory nature of jail relationships, but their place was willingly filled by Mohini, who mothered me, urged me not to sit on the cold ground, cooked for me, and generally fussed over me. My hair, now shoulder length, was dry and brittle from being washed with Lifebuoy soap, and at night she often massaged my scalp with coconut oil, telling me that this was what she did for her own daughter at home.

Since Kalpana had left, I had lost any remaining interest in cooking. I was quite happy to eat the Bihari village food that Mohini prepared for us. We used to eat a stodgy and filling porridge made from flour and salt and sometimes *khichri*, a mixture of lentils, rice and potatoes boiled up together. Strangely enough I did not gain any weight on this diet of carbohydrate. Sometimes Nago caught a pigeon and gave me a little of the curry, or one of the wardresses would bring a little piece of fish, a banana or some other titbit from her home. Though this diet was monotonous, it differed little from what most of my companions had been used to eating outside the jail. Their diet was regulated by seasonal availability. According to the time of year, they ate rice, millet or maize twice a day every day, with very little to accompany it.

Very few of them had even been able to afford tea, except on rare occasions. To Mohini and the others, my need for a morning cup of tea was a 'rich woman's' habit. This astonished me: I had always thought of India as the land of tea-drinkers, not realizing that tea, like many other products of a country that can grow more or less anything in one region or another, was beyond the budget of large sections of the Indian people. When we drank tea together, my companions often used to say that I was getting them into bad habits: they would never be able to afford to keep it up when they left jail.

The garden had been re-planted after the May rampage. But, though the work was done by prisoners, the produce was shared between matine and wardresses. I sometimes deliberately ignored this convention and helped myself and the other prisoners from the various plots. Probably to stop this, Nago had suggested that I have a little plot of my own. I planted garlic, coriander and tomatoes. As Christmas neared, I picked some of the riper-looking tomatoes and kept them between my blankets at night, hoping that the warmth of my body would redden them. I had not eaten a tomato for over a year and was impatient to taste them again. Sadly, the only result of my effort was a bag of squashed green tomatoes. The winter nights were long and the cold made me feel very hungry. The only snacks I could find were raw turnips, a thing I had never liked before, but now munched with relish.

The garden became very important to me. Its very greenness seemed to soothe me. The cold winter weather was ideal for digging, and I enthusiastically weeded and watered – the first gardening I had done since primary school. When the tomatoes did finally ripen, the children picked each day's crop and distributed it to all the prisoners in turn. Tomato chutney made a welcome change from the boiled turnips, radish or cauliflower leaves that were served up twice a day in that season. The red, sandy earth was amazingly fertile and things grew far more quickly than in England, but the problem was water, and it was often impossible to find enough.

On Christmas morning I made some watery rice pudding for the children, and persuaded a wardress to bring them a few boiled sweets. As I watched them sitting in my cell enjoying their 'party', I could not help contrasting their Christmas with that of children in Britain I had seen regaled with gifts and sweets. By this time, they had their own nickname for me, 'Merry Good', a version of my name combined with the only English they knew. I still made most fuss of Prokash, perhaps because his case was more tragic than the others. His crippled mother, abandoned by his father since being in jail, had brought him there as a two-day-old baby. His health disturbed me: his belly was distended, and, though the doctor could find nothing wrong with him, he often had fevers, and was unable to run and play with the other children as he quickly became breathless in the course of our games.

He was a very serious child. While I sat trying to read the Bengali books I had got the British consul to bring me, he used to sit quietly by my side, leafing through old copies of the Indian *Reader's Digest* as if he were absorbed in study. Sometimes I looked up to find him mimicking the postures and facial expressions of people in the photographs. He loved colour. Sometimes he came to me with a piece of rag he had found somewhere and asked me to 'embroider a flower' in it for him. I became so fond of him that I often thought of how I could adopt him, but sadly realized that it was futile to make such plans when my own future was so uncertain. His mother would have been glad to give him to me. She had already been in jail two years and the police had not even submitted her charge-sheet. When I left jail after five years, she was in exactly the same position and Prokash was six years old.

As the only literate female prisoner, I enjoyed unwarranted prestige. New prisoners frequently took me for the Superintendent; one asked me how much I earned! One day Bengia, a woman who had been transferred from another jail, asked me to read her palm. The only people she had known to keep books were astrologers, so she assumed that I also had visionary powers. Actually, all she wanted to know was whether the man she loved, said to be a member of a gang of robbers, was still keen on her. It was because she had refused to reveal his whereabouts to the police after two stolen sarees were found in her home that she had been arrested. She only stayed with us a short time. On the day she was to be taken back to Dhanbad, I heard the sounds of a heated argument coming from the dormitory. I ran to find out what was happening. Bengia was quarrelling with Prokash's mother, to whom she had given two rupees to pass on to a convict of her acquaintance who knew magic and would bring Bengia's lover back to her. Now, as the spell had not worked, Bengia was demanding her money back before leaving. The crippled woman protested that it was not her fault that Bengia was being transferred before the spell had time to work. Finally, an amicable settlement was reached, the money returned, and Bengia left.

Early in 1972, a young Santhal woman with a child in her arms joined us. She and her husband had both been arrested on a murder charge. The previous year their harvest had failed and they had borrowed money from a local moneylender, who also owned a large amount of land in their village. Every month, his agent called to collect an instalment of their repayment, at an interest rate of twelve and a half per cent per month. One day he turned up when her husband was out. There was no money in the house, and she told him to come back later. He refused to leave until she agreed to have intercourse with him in lieu of repayment. She was unwilling and he tried to rape her. As they were struggling, her husband arrived home and intervened. The moneylender's agent was killed in the fight.

In February 1972, I had another visit from the Deputy High Commission; the consul usually came every four or five months to see me. This time, he had not been able to bring the embroidery threads I had asked for; he said that was not really his line. He had however brought me two pencils, marked 'HM Government Property', and a shorthand pad stamped 'ER II'. For the first time, I was allowed to keep writing materials. I had also asked him for a Hindi dictionary to help me wade my way through the daily paper. Although I knew this could easily be obtained in Calcutta bookshops, he had not been able to find one. During the course of our conversation I realized that this was because he had assumed that I wanted it printed in the Roman script, not dreaming that I would bother to learn Devanagari, in which Hindi is written. It struck me as pointless to learn the language in an alphabet that would not even enable me to read the name of a railway station in some of the remoter areas, far less to decipher a newspaper. Possibly because they never spent long in one country, most of the British diplomats I encountered had little personal interest in India.

For the first time, I asked the consul to deposit with the Superintendent about one pound of the money that my father sent regularly to Calcutta for me, so that I could buy the embroidery materials and satisfy Prokash's desire for 'flowers'. I often used to worry about my dependence on my family and Amalendu's for my clothes, books and other needs. As far as possible I tried to emulate the other women by selling my rations and becoming 'self-sufficient'. It was not that my family and friends minded sending me anything; but I felt that those who had imprisoned me should not expect others to provide me with the necessities of life. As on previous occasions, I wrote a short letter to my parents, and asked the British official to assure them that I was perfectly well and that there was no need to worry. My father had offered to come to India, but I was not being hypocritical when I told him that I would prefer him not to do so: I knew that if he saw me in those conditions he would return to England even more worried about me, and that his visit would unsettle me too. More important, there was nothing he could do to help me; he would be allowed to meet me for an hour or so and would then have to leave me again. The total outcome of such a visit would be negative.

That winter, an old woman was carried into our ward one day by two warders. She had, literally, been sent to die from a small sub-jail where there were no medical facilities at all. As far as I could see, she was suffering from nothing more than dysentery, but this had been going on so long that she was very weak. She was lame and unable to move quickly to get to the latrine, so by the time she arrived her clothes were soiled and stinking. Nobody was willing to wash them. I myself was not very keen, but I realized that it was something that had to be done. We could not just let her die from neglect. Even if the doctor gave her medicine, any nursing would have to come from us. Every day for a week I boiled up her dirty clothes in an old pitcher, bathed her and rubbed her head with paraffin to get rid of the lice that had accumulated there as a result of several months of neglect. Mohini and some of the other women, seeing that it really was possible to save the old woman's life, joined in the work of looking after her. Within a fortnight, she had recovered sufficiently to hobble along to my cell so that I could put drops of oil in her ears, massage her back or cut her fingernails with the rusty blade that I had found in the garden. A month later, she had fully recovered, put on weight, and was beaming with happiness. Just to see her like that made every effort worthwhile. Right until the day she left us, she never ate anything without first calling me to share it with her. She used to call me the local equivalent of 'Whitey', to the amusement of the other prisoners.

It was about this time that I first became interested in the idea of using my time in jail to learn some basic medicine, which would be of use wherever I went. It was easier planned than done. It proved impossible to get any medical books. Over a year later, when I eventually did receive one book as a result of the efforts of my friend Ruth Forster in London, I found it largely inapplicable to the type of diseases and conditions that I was encountering. It was when I had some project such as this in mind that I most missed having access to libraries and bookshops. In jail, to get any programme of study started involved a protracted and tiring effort, repeated requests and long delays.

*The Times*, though it arrived irregularly and weeks late, did much to keep me mentally alive. At least I could follow major world events. I was very much affected by the National Liberation Front upsurge in Vietnam that Spring. Somehow it gave my spirits a tremendous lift to know that a just cause was on the way to victory. The Indian newspapers too sometimes carried significant revelations. One hundred and ninety-nine people had been killed by police bullets in the city of Calcutta in fifteen months. Ten students had been shot dead and 160 wounded in an incident in Bhagalpur Jail. Meantime the Congress Party was announcing a landslide victory in the March elections. I for one was not impressed. One of the wardresses told me that her husband had got fifteen rupees* for voting for the Congress. The labourers who were mending our walls in burning sun and hot winds were earning two rupees a day. The Congress budget that April announced a reduction in tax for the higher income brackets in order to discourage tax evasion. At the same time, the continuing presence of refugees from East Bengal was given as the excuse for raising the price of kerosene, an essential commodity in the Indian villages, where most homes had no electricity.

After the departure of Kalpana and Amalendu, some of the other Naxalite prisoners in Hazaribagh Jail took on the respon-

* I did not consider it meaningful in the context of this book to convert sums quoted in rupees into pounds sterling: for the reader's information, £1 at that time was equal to about eighteen rupees.

sibility of keeping in contact with me as far as jail conditions permitted. They were worried that I would become depressed if left alone. Occasionally I received a smuggled note from them. Although I did not know it at the time, the warders kept them well informed of my activities; one day I received a surprise letter telling me how much they appreciated my devotion to their country and the Indian people. I had not realized that what I did meant anything to people outside the walls of the female ward, and it inspired me to try to do better.

The censors did not conceal the reports of splits in the Naxalite movement which started appearing in the autumn of 1971. At first I was sceptical, but secret letters confirmed that there was an intensive ideological debate going on as a result of the serious setbacks that had been suffered since 1970. There were many points of discussion which would take a long time to resolve; meanwhile, various groups were continuing their separate activities in different parts of the country.

The convict who cleaned our latrines told me one morning that one of my co-defendants had contracted T B. The same man on another occasion whispered to me that he knew magic, and, if I gave him the magistrate's name and the address of the court where my case was pending, he would arrange bail for me. I told some of the other women in jest and was met with serious entreaties to try it. They proceeded to relate numerous instances where people had been released as a result of magic. One man was said to have fixed his eye on the Judge in such a way that the latter was compelled to acquit him, though he had committed murder.

On the whole we saw very little of the male prisoners, but sometimes at night we could hear them singing in the dormitories that lay just beyond our walls. Occasionally they would keep up a twenty-four hour chanting of religious songs, accompanied by the banging of their aluminium plates, that grew louder and quicker as the religious frenzy reached its climax. Leoni told me that some of the 'Untouchable' prisoners gave displays of dancing and female impersonation. Those prisoners wanting a performance would have to pay a warder to lock the

dancers in their dormitory for a night. Outside, too, street enter-
tainers generally came from these castes.

I never had the chance to address more than a superficial
remark even to the few male prisoners allowed into our ward on
essential business, as the warders kept strict watch. It was
obvious from the men's dry exhausted faces and thin bodies that,
apart from those privileged few who had found favour with the
authorities, they had to endure much harder conditions than
ours. I longed to ask them about their cases, their families and
their lives in jail, but it was impossible in those circumstances.

Letters from Britain brought news of my mother's serious ill-
ness. My father wrote that she was to enter hospital for a major
heart operation. Days were full and I was rarely alone or idle
for long enough to think much about my inability to help her,
but nights brought strange dreams and fantasies, in which
England and India were inextricably intermingled. Prisoners
from the jail would be sitting with my parents in our dining
room in Essex, or I would receive a parcel filled with a mixture
of Indian and English food. It seemed as if my subconscious
mind could not decide which country it belonged to. I wanted
the impossible: to be in both.

# 6. False Alarms

Early in March 1972, Amalendu's parents again made the difficult journey to visit me. This time they were not allowed to come inside the jail office; they stood outside, their anxious old faces looking at me through the thick metal mesh, trying to judge whether or not I had lost weight. They said that Amalendu and the other sixteen people who had been taken to Calcutta might be there for a long time, as the legal proceedings there showed no sign of being any more efficient than those in Bihar. This would delay our trial, and they wanted to apply for bail for me. According to the Indian Penal Code, bail may be granted to any female person, whatever the nature of the charges against her. After hearing their explanation, I signed the power of attorney enabling a lawyer to submit a bail petition for me, though I had little hope that it would be granted.

Several days afterwards, the Superintendent came to inform me that my court appearance had been fixed for 29 March in Jamshedpur. A letter from my father which arrived shortly after confirmed this. He said that the charge-sheet for the first case had been submitted and that for the second was in preparation. I was astounded. I had not even known that there was a second case. The Superintendent was as puzzled as I. One of the clerks, overhearing our conversation, confirmed that there were two warrants. He hunted them out. The second case, about which no one had bothered to inform me, involved far more extensive charges than the first, including waging war against the State, which can carry the death penalty. The dates on which I was supposed to have engaged in various conspiracies extended to 10 June 1970, at which time I had already been in jail nearly two weeks.

Within a few days of this unexpected development, I was again called to the office. Several plain-clothes police were there with the Superintendent, who acted as spokesman. He began by asking me what I thought about Naxalite politics, and whether I would engage in them if I were to be released. He then proceeded to utter devious warnings that Amalendu would very likely be hanged, and that, since I had 'been found in possession of so many arms', I would certainly receive a long sentence if I insisted on being brought to trial. He suggested that all this could be avoided if I either agreed to 'give up Naxalite politics' or to return to England, which would be far better for me than staying in jail. After listening for several minutes, I interrupted to ask exactly what he was trying to say. The verbal meandering resumed. Impatiently I inquired why, if the Indian Government thought it better for me to return to England, it had not sent me there two years previously. He then assured me that nobody wanted to force me to go, but it would be better for me. Tired of being a participant in this type of roundabout conversation that was obviously leading nowhere, I asked if I might return to my cell. That was the last I heard of that particular episode.

In the event, 29 March came and went without any more being said about taking me to court. I was not particularly surprised as I had been sceptical from the start. Nor was I really worried about the additional charges against me; by that time it had become obvious that the actual technicalities of one's detention made very little difference; one was detained at the government's pleasure, and would be released when the government saw fit. All the same, I was hurt when a letter arrived from my sister, of whom I was very fond, pleading with me to cooperate by going to court so that my case could soon be decided, and obviously implying that the delays were attributable to my own behaviour. I wrote trying to explain my helplessness to her, but knowing quite well that the letter would most probably never arrive. My inability to establish direct contact with friends and relatives at times like this was very upsetting. It was not until I returned to England and read the type of letters Foreign Office officials had been writing to my family that I understood their misinterpretation of my situation. One letter declared me to be 'set in my views and unrepentant', another expressed the view that it was 'for the best' that I was not allowed to meet Amalendu's family very often. In view of their efforts on my behalf and my dependence on them for clothing and other essentials, this seemed a particularly extraordinary comment to make.

What was true was that, understanding from the very first that it would be wrong to expect too much from the officials of the British High Commission, I confined myself to polite routine talks with them. But I never refused to go to court, be put on trial or to return to England, provided that no unprincipled conditions were imposed on me. On the contrary, I had several times complained to them that I was not being taken to court regularly, in accordance with Indian law. Their response had been to obtain an assurance from the Bihar Government that I was in fact being produced in court every fifteen days. In the circumstances, it was unrealistic to say the least to suppose that my fate was in my own hands.

At a further meeting in April that year with two representatives from the Deputy High Commission, the question of a separate trial was mooted, as it was obvious that those persons who had been taken to Calcutta would not be returning to Bihar in the near future. I asked for permission to consult those of my co-accused who were still in Hazaribagh. An early meeting was promised. As my teeth were troubling me, it was agreed at the same time that I would see a dentist. My complaints about the continuing irregularities in delivery of my mail were attributed by the British consul to the 'vagaries of the post'. He agreed to buy me some books I wanted with the money deposited by my father; the Superintendent said I could have anything that was not published in Peking. Some books sent by my friend Ruth Forster were also submitted to the Superintendent for censorship.

A month later, I had neither met my co-accused, received any books nor had any dental treatment. Promises made in the presence of British officials were almost invariably forgotten the minute they were out of sight. Mail continued to be agonizingly irregular. I had long ceased hoping to maintain regular contacts with friends and family. My own letters were delayed for weeks in the jail office before being sent out. Many disappeared forever. Sometimes I signed for a registered letter that had arrived in the office and had to wait impatiently for ten or fifteen days before, after many reminders, it was finally handed to me. I would be wondering all the time who had written and what the news was. I was at the mercy of lethargic, seemingly immovable, mean-minded bureaucrats.

Wardresses explained to me that the best way of moving the office staff was *ghush*, a bribe. They themselves had to give money to the clerks to make out their wage slips, refund their travelling allowances or even to withdraw money from their provident fund. One of them who had arranged her son's marriage was kept waiting for months and in the end had to pay twenty rupees for a withdrawal of five hundred. If they wanted a transfer to another jail, they bribed the appropriate clerk. If they wanted to reverse a transfer order, this could be accomplished by the same method.

The prisoners, too, suffered on account of the office staff's greed. Every so often, a 'transfer' scare would be raised. The word would be passed round that, for example, two hundred prisoners were to be moved to Buxar, over a hundred miles away. Everyone felt threatened, and all those who for various reasons did not want to be transferred, and who could afford it, would take the first opportunity of hurrying to the office clutching bundles of rupee notes to give to the Assistant Jailer in charge of the operation. Often it would turn out to be a complete hoax and nobody was transferred at all. But for eventualities such as this it was essential for prisoners to have money. Money alone could smooth one's path through the years of imprisonment. For this reason, the main efforts of most prisoners were concentrated on accumulating as much of it as possible, most of them by selling what was theirs or by performing certain tasks like washing clothes or cooking for other prisoners or staff, a minority by cunning and trickery.

In early June, shortly after the completion of my second year in prison, an Assistant Jailer came to tell me that the Deputy High Commission had sent a telegram asking for my decision about a separate trial. I replied that I wanted to apply for a trial for all those accused persons remaining in Hazaribagh, for legal aid, and, pending the start of the trial, for bail. They afterwards wrote to my father that I had replied 'ambiguously'. Meanwhile, Amalendu's family had submitted a bail petition for me, but it had not been heard.

On 10 June 1972, the Superintendent appeared for the first time in two months to inform me that I was to go to Jamshedpur next day for the start of my trial. Two large khaki bags were sewn in the tailors' workshop for me to carry my books and clothes in. That morning I had been issued with a week's rations, and I spent the whole afternoon making countless *chapatis* and a big saucepan of potato curry to distribute to all the prisoners as a farewell present. But, once again, the allotted day passed and I was still in Hazaribagh, not knowing what had gone wrong this time and left with hardly anything to eat for the rest of the week! On this latter count I had nothing to worry about because the other women gladly shared their food with me. It was several days before, after repeated questioning from me, an explanation for the false alarm was proffered. The Jailer said that, as seventeen people involved in the trial were in Calcutta, the magistrate had adjourned the hearing. A petition had been submitted for separation of the case against those of us in Hazaribagh from that of the accused in Calcutta.

The next news I had of the case was in August. One Sunday afternoon at about five o'clock an Assistant Jailer came to my cell with a notification that I should arrange for a lawyer to represent me at a hearing in Patna High Court to take place on the following day. The Prosecution had submitted a petition for the transfer of the trial to Hazaribagh itself, stating that the restricted accommodation in Jamshedpur Jail and the Naxalite activities taking place in that area would make it a grave security risk to take us there. At that short notice it was impossible even to get as far as the jail office to speak to the Jailer or Superintendent, let alone to contact people in Calcutta who might be able to arrange legal representation. The distances involved were far too great for anything effective to be done. In the event, the petition was never heard and, many months later, was withdrawn altogether, because, by that time, Naxalite activities had spread to Hazaribagh District too. In the meantime, all court hearings were stayed.

After the disastrous rains of 1971, 1972 brought drought and a tormenting heatwave. On awakening each morning, my first thought was to scan the morning sky anxiously for any signs of cloud that might bring the rain we needed so desperately. Mosquitoes made the hours from dusk to dawn a nightmare. My face was red and swollen and I had a permanent headache from lack of sound sleep. In the morning, my clothes and the saree I used for a sheet were blood-bespattered like a miniature battlefield. Worse, our water supply dwindled to a yellowish trickle. We gave up trying to grow anything in our garden. The worst times were when our tap dried up altogether, sometimes for several days, and we had to manage with two buckets of water between four of us for bathing, washing our clothes, cooking and cleaning. The other women were far worse off; all they had were a few pitchers and a couple of rusty buckets between all of them. The water butt had long since started leaking and had been discarded. To make matters worse, many of the warders were reluctant to go to the bother of arranging for convicts to fetch water for us from the only two wells in the jail that had not dried up. Some of them had almost to be prayed to for a bucket of water.

There was even more sickness than usual among the prisoners that year. One of my cellmates was suffering from malaria, and even on those hot and sultry nights would shiver under all the blankets we could muster. I could feel my own health deteriorating. I suffered repeated attacks of vomiting and was often unable to eat for whole days at a time. The doctors did not take it seriously, putting my physical condition down to my mental state. In the end I myself began to wonder if it was all caused by anxiety over my mother's sickness, the poor conditions Amalendu was being kept in, or the general uncertainties of my own situation.

The children too had all manner of intestinal troubles. One day Murti, the little girl whose marriage had been arranged, had a particularly severe attack of vomiting and diarrhoea. The convict in charge of medicines gave her mother a tablet, telling her to give the child a quarter of it. In her anxiety to make her daughter better, she thought it would have more effect if she gave Murti the whole pill. Murti was unconscious for almost two days. On the second afternoon I was lying down after one of my usual bouts of sickness when the mother, Balko, came to my cell and, apologizing for disturbing me, told me Murti was asking for me. The woman was crying bitterly, afraid that her child would die as a result of her foolish action. I hurried to the dormitory where Murti was lying, still semi-conscious, on the matine's bed. Her normally bright and cheeky face was pale and hollow, her eyes sunken into their sockets. She turned her head towards me, her eyes moved in recognition, weakly she stretched her hand towards me and motioned to me to lie beside her. Tears filled my eyes when the women told me that her first words on recovering consciousness had been to ask for me. Although I had to be locked up separately at night, I spent the next few days at her bedside until she had recovered sufficiently for me to wrap her in a blanket and carry her out to see what remained of the garden where we had worked together.

Other children were not so lucky. One day, a young woman arrived from Chatra, a sub-jail about thirty miles from Hazaribagh, bearing in her arms the skeleton of a child, still breathing but beyond cure. His limbs were like dry twigs, his big tragic eyes bulged from a head over which the skin was drawn tightly like a membrane. His elbows, knees and ankles were covered in sores, his hands and feet white and bloodless; bags of wrinkled skin hung from his armpits and his hollow buttocks. He clutched and clawed feebly at his mother's breast, as if trying to find a way back into the protection of the womb. He had not even the strength to cry. He had been suffering from diarrhoea for two months and, as there were no medical facilities in Chatra, had become progressively weaker. Finally, on seeing, presumably, that he was going to die, the Jailer there had swiftly arranged to have him transferred to Hazaribagh, ostensibly for 'treatment'. Two days later, just when I was holding him to give his mother a rest, he died. I was overcome with grief and resentment at the unnecessary death. This corpse of an eighteen-month old boy was the first I had ever seen. I looked on, numb and disconsolate, as the sweepers, members of the Harijan community who do all the work of corpse disposal, wrapped the bony little body in a piece of cloth and took it to be burned by the side of the lake just beyond the jail walls. For my fellow prisoners, the incident, though sad, had none of the significance that it did for me; in the hard lives they had led, premature deaths were almost an everyday occurrence.

Shortly after this the Superintendent visited us again, in the company of a local official. I asked him to arrange my transfer to Jamshedpur so that I could find out what was happening with regard to my case. His reaction was almost violent: 'Be careful how you speak to me or you'll find all your teeth knocked out!' And then he said, 'Why don't all you Naxalites rot and die in jail? I'm fed up with all of you.' I realized that something must have happened in the male sector to upset him, and some days later I found out what. The inquiry into the 1971 shooting had started. The investigating judge had inspected the Naxalite wards and had been greeted with shouted slogans of, 'We will take blood for blood,' and this had infuriated the Superintendent.

Just before the anniversary of the shooting there was a further order from the 'Super' for all trees and bushes to be cut down. The jasmine had started blossoming again, though sparsely, and the guavas were sending out new shoots. The margosa had grown new branches and was providing us with a little shade again. Now, all was taken from us once more. On 25 July the male Naxalites shouted slogans for hours on end. The wind that day was coming from the south, and bore their resounding shouts to our ears. They were keeping up the challenge in the best way they could. That same month the newspapers brought word of the death in police custody a few days after his arrest, of Charu Mazumdar, the first General Secretary of the Marxist-Leninist Communist Party of India, the party which had been formed in 1969, and had given the main leadership to the Naxalite movement. It was widely thought that he had been killed by the police. What I found cynically amusing was that the censors never bothered to cut any news that they thought might help to demoralize us. However, these tactics had the opposite effect on me. I automatically considered every part of the paper that they blacked out as being good news, and the more they blacked out, the happier I was.

At the beginning of September I fell so ill that I was unable to get up at all. I felt weak as never before, I had lost two stone in weight, and the doctor in charge of our ward was still unable to diagnose the cause. Every day he came to urge me to eat, but the sight of food repelled me. I had lain there for a week, my body racked with fever, when the other jail doctor was called and immediately diagnosed hepatitis. For a short time I became a VIP; they were genuinely afraid of being held responsible if anything happened to me. I was comparatively well known, people outside were asking about me, and they could not cover up what happened to me as they could with many other prisoners. For one month I enjoyed the luxury of a bed and mosquito net and was regaled with nutritious food that I was too sick to eat.

My fellow-prisoners did all they could to nurse me back to health, massaging me, fanning me, washing my clothes, cleaning my cell, preparing rice gruel, or just coming to ask how I was feeling. One said to me: 'You are a long way from home, and that is making you feel worse. But you must remember that now we are your mother, your sister, your family. We will take care of you.'

I felt then that a qualitative change had come over my relationship with my companions. Lying on my bed on those late September days, I felt at peace as I idly watched the women moving to and fro, the clear sky where white clouds were jostling for attention, the cranes flying to their nests in the peepul trees, the children playing under the margosa tree. But never for long.

Even when I was ill, a surprise search was conducted, blankets and mattress shaken out, newspapers unfolded. What they expected to find at a time when I could hardly stand up, I do not know.

I was still quite weak when three schoolmistresses joined us for several days. They and several thousand schoolmasters had been arrested during the course of a strike after the imposition of Section 144 of the Indian Penal Code banning processions and meetings of more than five people. They were demanding government takeover of the private schools they worked in, so as to have some security with regard to pension, housing, and, more important, regular payment of salaries. They told me that they were sometimes not paid for months on end. In order to cope with the influx of prisoners, the government reopened an old prison camp at Chandwara, about twenty miles from Hazaribagh, which had, I think, first been used by the British. Chandwara and other prison camps were used with increasing regularity in the years that followed. The schoolteachers were the first of many waves of strikers I saw in jail. Though that time they were relatively easily demoralized and released after agreeing to an unconditional return to work, later strikes were not put down so quickly.

That was the only time that strikers were given a higher classification and better food than the other prisoners. They also, much to my annoyance, received a full issue of clothing, which they took with them on leaving. The reason for my disgruntled feelings was that some of the other women were, as usual, walking around in rags. After the schoolteachers had gone, I had a major row with the Assistant Jailer in charge of clothing. Some of the women had not even a blouse to cover their thin shoulders, and, with the cool weather coming, were already in difficulties. After a perfunctory inspection the officer decreed that those who had nothing at all would be issued with a saree and blouse. Nothing else. I contrasted this with what had been given to the schoolmistresses, who were already well provided with their own clothing and were only there for a few days anyway. He explained that my companions were poor even before they came to jail;

outside too they often had to wear rags, and could not expect to 'get rich' in jail custody. The fact that many people outside had to get through the harsh winter months barefoot and without sufficient clothing seemed to him justification enough for depriving prisoners even of the minimal necessities they should have received according to jail rules. And the Congress Government had won the elections on the slogan 'Away With Poverty!'

It was common knowledge that the Assistant Jailer and the convicts in his charge were selling the prisoners' clothing quotas and entering in the books that the things they sold for their own profit had been issued to prisoners. The only time clothing was ever supplied without a prolonged struggle was when a visit of a Minister or the Inspector General for Prisons was announced. Then, hastily, the Jailer would hand out a few blouses or sarees to those who looked most ragged, and warn the others not to complain, assuring them that he would see to them 'as soon as the new stocks arrived'; this promise was promptly forgotten as soon as the dignitary had departed.

When I had more or less recovered from jaundice, a British official once more came to see me, bringing a long-awaited pen, and, unexpectedly, an offer of 'voluntary repatriation' without trial which, he said, the Indian Government would almost certainly agree to if I was willing. I said I would consider the matter and asked him to give me a month to make up my mind.

# 7. Repatriation?

The Deputy High Commission secretary's proposal was tempting: if I agreed to voluntary repatriation, he felt optimistic that the case against me would be withdrawn; I could virtually walk out tomorrow. On the other hand, if I insisted on waiting for a trial, it could take months. The Bihar Government considered me 'dangerous', would oppose any bail attempts on my behalf and had warned again that, if tried, I should be sentenced to twenty years' imprisonment. The British official thought it unrealistic to hope that I should ever be able to see Amalendu again. The Superintendent at that point mentioned casually that there would probably be several death sentences in our case, but by now I knew that this was just an attempt to frighten me. The consul departed with a final piece of information given him by the Bihar Chief Secretary: if ever I attempted to live in Calcutta, my life would be in danger. The situation was not what it had been in 1970. Naxalites would not be tolerated.

This thinly veiled threat did not impress me. I doubted whether people in Calcutta had anything against me. I tried to consider the repatriation proposal logically, unmoved by emotional considerations. It was obvious that the Indian Government had not had a change of heart. Their apparent willingness to release me was designed to enhance their image abroad, while enabling them to continue the indefinite detention without trial of thousands of their political opponents at home. Even so, I concluded that it was to my advantage to accept the offer. No purpose could be served by remaining in jail any longer. Some days afterwards I received a message from some of the men in my case, advising me to agree to repatriation, provided no unacceptable conditions were attached. I was glad they had written to me; I did not want to leave behind me the impression that I was running away.

Within two weeks, I had made up my mind and wrote to Calcutta asking them to go ahead with the proposed negotiations. The jail officers seemed so certain that I would soon be on my way to England that the initial doubts I had as to whether the whole thing would really come off soon diminished. Letters from my closest friends in England made me think longingly of life in London, and I was looking forward to seeing my parents and especially my sister's children. On the other hand, the thought of leaving India for good was painful. As I relaxed in the clear autumn afternoons on the raised mud platform we had made outside our cell, looking up into the pure blue of the Hazaribagh sky, watching the vultures circling lazily over the corpse-burning ground outside the jail, breathing in the fragrance of earth and air still sweet from the monsoon rains, I felt sad that these days were to be my last in the country I had come to love from inside jail walls. Thinking that I might never see Amalendu again, I made practical plans for keeping in touch with his family, and wrote explaining what had happened. I knew that he would understand.

Outside, India was seething. That autumn there were riots over language in Assam, massive student unrest in Punjab, and daily disturbances reported from other parts of the country. One day a lady member of the Bihar Legislative Assembly was brought to jail after being arrested in the course of a sit-down protest in Ramgarh, thirty miles south of Hazaribagh. Though she was with us only a couple of days, her short sojourn was enlightening. She was the member for Ramgarh, a seat previously held by her husband, who had been assassinated in Patna shortly after his election. The Communist Party of India had decided that she should run in his place, and emotional pull had seen her elected. I was interested to discuss politics with her. She had never heard of Marx, Engels, or Lenin. When I asked her about her governmental work, she confessed that, as she knew very little English, she could not understand all the proceedings of the Legislative Assembly.

I told her of the plight of prisoners who were held without trial for long periods, and described our difficulties to her. She showed only minimal interest, as if it were something which did not really concern her. She was more interested in hearing about English cooking and knitting patterns. Moreover, her arrival coincided with the start of Ramadan, the Muslim month of fasting and I was somewhat amused to see this 'Communist' lady dutifully observing her dawn to dusk fast, quite unaware that there was anything incongruous about it.

One of my former schoolteaching colleagues, Iris Marks, was in India with her husband and had written to me many months before that they would try to visit me. As the time passed and they did not appear I had given up hope of seeing them. One day in late October that year I was called to the office. Iris had arrived, having obtained the necessary permission from the Central Government. They wanted to stay a week in Hazaribagh and see me every day, but these plans were thwarted by the Superintendent, who announced that only one visit would be allowed. They had made a detour of several hundred miles for this dubious favour. I felt guilty about it, but they assured me it was worthwhile. From my point of view, it was marvellous, even though spontaneity was somewhat blunted by the presence of the inevitable Special Branch man who sat, quite expressionless, taking note of our every word. The Superintendent was in one of his most officious moods, as if he begrudged us our exuberant chatter. I had written asking Iris to bring a small rubber ball with her, as the children had asked me to get one for them. Now he decided that, as I was not allowed to play with the children, neither the ball nor the sweets Iris had brought for them would be 'passed'.

Luckily, he did allow me to keep the things that Iris and Peter had brought for me personally. After my recovery from hepatitis, my interest in food had revived. In fact I was so obsessed by it at that time that, whenever a consignment of English newspapers arrived, instead of looking for news from home, I immediately hunted out all the cookery columns and started planning how I could make versions of the recipes given there from my jail rations. Not that I got far in practice. Resources were too limited to make anything remotely resembling the tasty dishes described. The sweets, fresh fruit, and tins of cheese that Iris and Peter had bought me were like the fulfilment of a dream.

Soon, however, they were causing the same old conflict of mind and matter, and I wrote to her: 'The sweets were delicious, but I feel awful whenever I have any luxury. I usually distribute it to get rid of it quickly and then still feel guilty for the bit I ate. I suppose when I'm back in London I'll be able to eat a normal meal without feeling like a predatory and loathsomely rich glutton. Till then I'm probably better off with my *chapatis* and lentil soup.'

Understanding my need for creativity in my humdrum jail existence, Iris had brought me cloth and threads to embroider a smock, and some pastels and drawing paper. Though she asked me several times what they could do for me, I was expecting to be repatriated in a short time and could not think of anything in particular. I promised her I would soon be seeing her in our old London haunts. Three years later when I was back in England, I discovered that both Iris and Peter had been frisked before meeting me and that, in Calcutta, after Iris had been to see Amalendu in court, the police had come to their hotel and taken her to the police station for questioning.

That autumn we were joined by several young and energetic prisoners, and in the afternoons we often played hide-and-seek, *kobbody*, a rough kind of tag, hopscotch and long-jump. The one who did most to brighten our lives was Bilkish, a Muslim girl of nineteen who had eloped with a Hindu youth from her neighbourhood after a secret romance conducted by means of love-letters and messages conveyed by servants. Now both of them had been imprisoned at the instigation of her guardian, an uncle, supported by members of the Muslim community, who threatened to lynch the couple if they dared to show their faces in their home district. For fear of communal riots, the magistrate refused them bail, saying that their lives would be in danger if they were released.

Bilkish's husband had been charged with abduction and rape, a charge that could never hold water unless the girl herself made a statement that he had carried her off against her will. She was subjected to intensive medical examinations to establish her age; any female under eighteen was considered a minor and needed a guardian's consent to marry. But Bilkish was clearly old enough to choose her own husband. She told me that as she was about to finish her schooling, her uncle had arranged her marriage to a cousin; it was to avoid this that she had eloped with the man she loved. Bilkish had tremendous spirit and I could not but admire her determination in standing up to all threats from her uncle, who came to visit her every day until she refused to meet him any more. After that he managed to persuade one of the Assistant Jailers to represent his case to the girl. This officer came frequently to our ward to utter predictions of the future unhappiness that awaited a woman who married outside her own community. He warned her that the Hindu family she had married into would never eat anything she cooked nor drink water from receptacles touched by her. He tried his best in every way to demoralize and discourage her so that she would relent and make a false statement against her husband that could bring him a ten-year jail sentence for rape, and agree to return to her uncle's household, where she could be sure of being suitably punished for her 'crime'.

The couple had friends as well as enemies among the jail staff but the former were, if anything, even more unpleasant characters. They were a couple of old Brahman warders, notorious among the prisoners for their tyranny and general contempt for the well-being of their charges. In contrast with their behaviour towards the rest of us, they did all they could to assist Bilkish and her husband and make jail life easy for them. As far as I could see, their reason for doing so was that they saw Bilkish's marriage into a Hindu family as a victory for their religion and a gain from the Muslims. They would have been furious and quite unrelenting if their own daughters had wanted to marry outside their caste. Despite the pressures from various sources, Bilkish remained adamant and stood her ground for five months before being released and allowed to join her husband, on condition that they went to live in another area. The irony of it all was that, according to law, India is a secular state, and they had committed no crime whatsoever.

After Mohini's release on bail, my cell was shared for a time by two women from the Ganjhu caste, Rajkumari and Somri. I had great respect for Rajkumari. Like most of the tribal people I met, she hated quarrels, was hard-working and very straight-forward. There was no guile about her; she was completely trust-worthy. In the evening after we were locked up she would stand silent for a few minutes by the bars. It was at that time every day that she remembered her home and her village. Somri would then call her to eat and forget her troubles. At nights, she some-times used to sing village songs. Try as I might, I was unable to learn to reproduce the plaintive yet harmonious vibrations of her powerful and melodious voice. I never met any prisoner who could sing so well.

Somri was a good-natured widow of about thirty-five with a son of about fifteen who was also in jail. She was very warm-hearted and always called me the 'kid'. She cooked for me, scrubbed my back when I had a bath and covered me with her own blankets in the cold winter nights. Scared of insects, frightened of ghosts, she was born to be on the receiving end of prac-tical jokes. In her motherly company I seemed to become more childish and sometimes my stomach would ache with laughter after hiding my hairbrush in her bed or convincing her that there was a ghost in the latrine, so that she remained in agony for hours rather than enter the haunted place. She never lost her temper. Her appearance was somewhat comical. Like many vil-lage women, she wore a small gold ring in her nose. It hung directly above a gap in her front teeth, which she once told me was the result of a stumble in the dark one night when she had been drinking country liquor and was carrying a sack of rice on her head.

Like three-quarters of India's peasants, she came from an area where the only irrigation was rain. Farming consisted mainly of paddy, millet and maize cultivation; this meant planting and leaving the rest up to 'god'. The only diet she had known were these cereals and whatever the jungle provided in the way of edible leaves, roots, fruit and flowers. She had never eaten onions or potatoes before coming to jail and had not even heard of common foods like bananas and coconuts. Yet, despite her limited experience, she was very shrewd. She did not entertain a high opinion of government officials, who sometimes used to go to their village to recruit youths for the army, to die for the 'big people', as she put it, or to tell them not to have too many children or promise them land – a promise which had never been fulfilled. The government she saw as a remote body that prevented the villagers from collecting firewood in the jungle or fishing in the ponds, and made them grow cotton where they needed rice.

Like some other prisoners, the only two foreign countries Somri had heard of were Pakistan and China. She had heard that the Chinese either eat or kill all their old people, and that they eat snakes and monkeys, which she considered holy creatures. I told her what I knew about China and explained the long struggle that people there had gone through to transform the old society. Recalling the anti-China propaganda I had seen displayed on station bookstalls and in other places since the first day I crossed the border into India, I began to think that the strange stories I heard about China from Somri and from other people, were more than just coincidence.

Our talks were not confined to politics. One night she told me a hair-raising tale of how her nephew had been mauled and killed by a tiger when collecting firewood. There were still many wild animals in some districts of Bihar and I could not help contrasting the village people's dangerous existence with the easy life I had always taken for granted. She also described to me how, in the month of April, the villagers spent every day from dawn to dusk gathering the fallen flowers of the *mohua* tree which, dried in the sun, stored, and later boiled or roasted, formed their staple diet for several months and were eaten twice a day until the maize was ready in July. Every member of the family joined in this work and there was no time even to have a bath, because that entailed walking a long way to the nearest water. She said she always got lice in the *mohua* season because there just wasn't time to keep clean.

Most of the time Somri earned her keep by running a shop for a local moneylender. All she received was food and, occasionally, clothing for herself and her son. She was in jail for having supplied provisions to a gang of *dacoits* or robbers who roamed the area, pouncing now and again on people going to and from market, or raiding the homes of those who were away for some reason. Some of the *dacoits* themselves had been arrested in their jungle hideout and three of their wives were with us for several months. They were Pahariyas, members of a hill tribe which, by tradition, engages in roving cultivation, moving from one place to another every few seasons. They were very timid and it was difficult to imagine them living rough in the forests with their husbands on the proceeds of their raids.

The eaves of the small hut opposite our cell were inhabited by a pair of pigeons which produced young at incredibly frequent intervals. The meat of these young birds, when about ten days old, was much coveted by the meat-starved prisoners, but was usually considered the prerogative of the matine. We developed a system whereby we sometimes managed to magic away the young pigeons before the matine even realized they were there. Saturday was our night for secret feasts. Just before locking time, when nobody was looking, one of us would stand guard while the other two smuggled our mud fire into the cell, where it remained concealed on the latrine step until the Chief Head Warder had completed his evening round. As soon as he was out of sight the cooking would start. When there was no pigeon, we made potato *khichri* or got one of the wardresses to bring us some seasonal vegetables from the market. When I lay down to sleep after these feasts I always thought of Amalendu and wondered whether he had any company or not; but I knew that, whatever his own condition, he would not want me to be unhappy and would be glad to know that I was 'managing'.

\*

Just before Christmas 1972 there was an influx of non-gazetted employees of the Bihar government, mostly mental home nurses and hospital workers, on strike for better pay, free medical treatment and improved housing. They had been arrested on the familiar charge of violating Section 144 by demonstrating in support of their demands.

As usual when large numbers of new prisoners arrived, our feelings were mixed. We liked the variety they introduced into our lives, but on the other hand felt keenly the increased difficulties, caused by lack of water and poor sanitation. Now there were eighty of us all competing for water from the same spluttering tap, and thirty-four women sleeping in the cell next to mine. There was never a moment's quiet. I abandoned all attempts at study and spent my time watching and chatting with the new inmates. Being members of a union, they were militant and organized, and plagued the Chief Head Warder incessantly with their demands. Their boldness in approaching the authorities was an example for other prisoners, who also began to raise their voices in protest, particularly about the food. The daily vegetable at that time was aubergine, boiled in an iron drum till it was black and slimy. Worst of all, fat red worms were frequently found in it, so that most women preferred to eat plain rice or *chapatis* rather than inadvertently chew one of these 'delicacies'.

Mental home nursing, hospital cleaning and menial work were considered undesirable and unclean occupations, and most of the 'NGOs' were either Christians or Harijans. There was, however, among these rough and ready types one notable exception, a Hindu woman who was a *bhoktin* or devotee. I am not sure how she came to acquire this exalted position. She was supposed to enjoy special powers as a clairvoyante and confidante of the gods, and before eating she always performed complicated rituals. She would not touch food cooked by non-Hindus or Harijans, so most of the NGOs sat idle while she and a few 'acceptable' women prepared the food. Everyone had to keep at a distance when she approached the tap with her pitcher, for fear of defiling her water. One morning she tipped away a whole bucketful because Somri had accidentally brushed against it. After cooking, she had to eat first and separately, and all her utensils were kept apart from the others so as to avoid mixing them up.

I was becoming ever more aware of the power of caste in the supposedly secular state of India. I had previously had no idea at all of the ramifications of the caste system, naïvely believing, as I had read in history books, that there were only four Hindu castes, not realizing that these are subdivided into an estimated two thousand five hundred, each of which marries only within its own community, according to elaborate rules. Each caste has strict regulations as to which other castes it can associate with, and to what degree. Rajkumari told me that outside she could never eat rice cooked by anyone but a Brahman or a member of her own community, though she would eat dry food prepared by certain other castes.

One of the old Hindu wardresses, despite long years of jail service, still insisted on adhering to all her taboos. She flatly refused to sleep on a bed which had been used by anyone who ate meat, fish or eggs, or to eat food cooked on a fire where these things were also cooked. Whenever any of us trapped a pigeon we had to make sure that she did not come to know about it; nothing could have been better calculated to make her rant and rave about our wickedness. She would not touch any of the prisoners' clothing and kept all her blankets and bedding rolled up in a corner, where nobody would 'contaminate' it. Provision had to be made for the night wardresses to sleep inside the jail because, once the gate of the female ward was locked from outside when the Chief Head Warder left at six o'clock, they had no way of getting out until six the next morning.

Whenever a new prisoner arrived, one of the first questions from those who curiously crowded round her would be, '*Kya jat hai?*' (What caste are you?) Once this piece of valuable information was given, all her behaviour could thereafter be accounted for by the fact that she belonged to this or that community. The preconceived ideas of characteristics and qualities peculiar to particular castes were, presumably, no more accurate than the ideas of an English person who says all the Scots are mean and all the Irish lazy!

On the whole, caste was never a big issue in my relations with the other women. They were good-humoured and tolerant towards what they must often have seen as my strange and un-orthodox behaviour. Once or twice, however, I did encounter the disapproval of Hindu purists on the jail staff. One of the few things the Chief Head Warder knew about Britain was that people there eat beef; occasionally he would 'tut tut' as he looked at me, then shake his head and say, '*Bohut kharap jat*' (Very bad caste). I was glad that he regarded me with distaste; at least it meant that he kept his covetous eyes off the sweets and other edibles that visitors sometimes brought me. Once, a British High Commission visitor, perhaps somewhat tactlessly, brought me a tin of Corned Beef and a jar of Bovril. They could not be passed because the Special Branch police who had to check all items brought by outsiders were orthodox Hindus and refused to touch them.

An example of how caste rigidity could serve the purposes of those elements in society who wanted, for whatever reason, to hinder progress, was given me by one of the wardresses, who said that in her village the Brahmans, members of the 'highest' Hindu caste, had warned the people not to send their children to the local school where some of the teachers were Christians and Harijans; contact with these people would make them 'lose caste'.

The NGOs brightened my Christmas that year. The Chris-tians among them danced and sang in the yard outside my cell from early morning until the Warder came to lock up for the night. A couple of days after the holiday I found, concealed in some rations delivered to me, a crumpled note addressed to 'My dear sister', offering to help me in any way I wanted. This un-expected missive led to a touching friendship with one of the young male convicts who sometimes came to our ward. He told me that the few sweets I had given him on Christmas morning had moved him to run the risk of writing to me. If the note had been discovered, he would probably have been beaten, certainly fettered and put in solitary. In the event, we continued our correspondence regularly and undiscovered for several months.

Shortly after we started writing, his baby daughter died. When he was due for release, the Assistant Jailer in charge of that particular job asked him for twenty-five rupees, the price, he said, of one month's remission. If he could not pay, he would have to stay in jail a month more. After his child's death he was anxious to get back to his wife, and paid up. The day he departed, I felt as if I had lost a brother.

Through his boldness I had also been able to keep in touch with some of the Naxalite prisoners in near-by wards, and had learned that one of them, Ashim Chatterjee, was being kept in solitary confinement, in the condemned cell, fettered, and with no other company than the two warders and one head warder who were on constant duty there. While the Indian Government was making a great hue and cry that Sheikh Mujibur Rahman was not allowed a radio in jail in Pakistan, Ashim was not even allowed a pencil and paper to occupy himself. This practice of keeping political prisoners in the condemned cell before they had been tried seemed to me the ultimate mockery of the tenet that a man is innocent until he is proved guilty.

Eventually, the government employees withdrew their strike and were released, though some had lost their jobs for defying the government's original order to return to work, and the rest would not be paid for the days they had missed. Materially, they had gained nothing; but the government was nonplussed by the continuing waves of strikes and other disturbances. In the jail itself, life was becoming more and more anarchic with increasingly frequent overnight influxes of large numbers of prisoners of a different type from those the jail authorities had been used to bullying. These new prisoners were militant, united, sure of their rights and not afraid to fight for them. They were a constant headache for a jail administration caught between the government's instructions to make no concessions to the militants and the prisoners' own demands as to how they were to be treated. The jail officers solved this problem by entering the jail as seldom as possible so as not to come face to face with these troublesome types who just would not keep quiet.

Despite the mounting physical difficulties caused by overcrowding, I welcomed the new situation for two reasons; first, the new prisoners were the living proof of the Indian people's fighting spirit; second, they took the authorities' mind off the rest of us and consequently we enjoyed a measure of relaxation in our daily lives.

Tension was, however, never far below the surface and, shortly after the N G Os' departure, I received a sudden shaking up. One morning, some of the women told me they had been having a discussion in the dormitory the night before. Many of them had been detained several years without trial and, as there were no signs of any developments in their court cases, were in despair of ever being released. They had decided to go on hunger strike from that day, mainly to demand a speedy settlement of their cases, but also for certain improvements in jail food and facilities. I warned them that, whatever happened, they must remain united and not allow themselves to be intimidated by the threats and bullying of the warders; otherwise they would achieve nothing at all. I agreed to join the hunger strike.

That morning everyone except the matine refused the daily chick peas and molasses, and since the Chief Head Warder was on holiday, his deputy, a lean and hard man, was called to settle the dispute. His first words on entering our ward were, 'What is that Naxalite doing with the other prisoners? She has taught them to do this. Lock her in her cell!' He was referring, of course, to me. I said nothing, leaving it to one of the other women to state our demands. Even as she started speaking, the warder began to brush aside her words and repeat his order that I should be locked up. The woman who had spoken was also locked up, after which he proceeded to shout at and abuse the others, telling them how ungrateful they were to the government which, despite all their crimes, was feeding them and sheltering them. How could they dare to complain? After more in this vein, the women agreed, one by one, to eat their chick peas and forget the hunger strike. The warder departed with a final warning to them not to associate with Naxalites, and, although he allowed a wardress to unlock my cell, he gave instructions that nobody was to talk to me.

That evening, when the lean warder came to lock us, Bilkish deliberately took hold of my hand in front of him and said, 'Come on, Didi, let's walk round the garden once more before locking.' Rajkumari and Somri had already refused to make the bed of the only wardress who tried to obey the warder's instructions to keep them away from me, and made up their minds not to talk to her. I told them not to be childish, she was only doing her duty, but secretly I could not help being impressed by their defiance of officialdom.

I judged from this episode that the Naxalite spectre was still haunting the government, though it had claimed to have wiped out the movement completely. Pieces of information gleaned from various sources confirmed my suspicion that the Naxalites were very much in existence. Several times the Home Minister assured the government that a 'close watch' was being kept on 'extremists'. Rifle-snatching incidents were reported from North Bengal, and special police camps set up to encircle the Kankse area in Burdwan District, West Bengal, where Naxalites had been particularly successful in mobilizing the tribal people against feudal landlords who held them in slavelike bondage. Siddharta Sankar Ray, the Chief Minister of Bengal, urged his police to befriend the villagers and win them over, but after the terror that the rural population had witnessed in 1970 and 1971, it was too late for that. Though it might take a long time to recover the ground that had been lost after the intense revolutionary wave of 1967–9, things were on the move again.

By this time, the government was making wide use of its powers under the Maintenance of Internal Security Act, and other preventive detention laws. One day the Calcutta *Statesman* reported that 775 people had been detained under the MISA in three months in the State of Bengal alone. By the beginning of 1973, too, riots had broken out in the state of Andhra Pradesh in the south. People there had burned railway stations and post offices and had attacked units of the army and the Central Reserve Police sent to quell them. The situation throughout the country was explosive.

I had almost forgotten about the repatriation scheme when,

one day, I had another visit from Calcutta. The Deputy High Commission secretary assured me that they were still doing their best and that things were 'moving in the right direction'. The 'wheels of government' were causing delays, but he was optimistic that there would soon be a positive development. Would I suggest who would pay my air fare? I was reluctant to ask my friends or family for the money, particularly as the police had seized money of mine from Calcutta. However, when the British official indicated that, unless I found somebody to pay my fare, the whole project would be abandoned, I wrote a note to my friend Ruth Forster in London, asking her to make the money available. On return to London years later I heard from her that the Foreign Office had asked her to be on call night and day with the money. She had been so sure that I was coming home that she had even bought me some new slippers!

For several months after this I heard nothing further. I put the idea of a quick return to Britain to the back of my mind. Occasionally when a letter from friends or family or a dream made it come to the fore again, I felt furious with the High Commission people for ever having mentioned the repatriation plan in the first place. My parents, Ruth and other friends were, if anything, more anxious than I and my mother was still in poor health after her operation. Once I wrote to the Deputy High Commissioner himself inquiring what had become of the scheme and requesting him not to abandon it. Perhaps he never received my letter; in any case, I got no reply.

February 1973 saw the return of two prisoners I had seen released on bail over two years previously, Budhni, a young woman of about twenty-five, and her old mother-in-law. Budhni's husband had been in jail since the time of their arrest, but they had not been able to afford to come and visit him for over a year. The two women had been re-arrested for 'jumping bail'; they had not been able to find the six rupees it cost to travel by bus from their home to Hazaribagh for their court appearance. They had sold their land, their household goods and their jewellery to raise money to try to settle their case, which involved charges of keeping unlicensed firearms. In the end they had been left destitute and the case had still not been heard in court. The two women had spent the past year doing menial jobs from house to house in order to survive. Their return to prison made me feel very depressed.

By the time the Hindu Holi festival arrived in March, I had still received no word about my repatriation. Six months had elapsed since the original proposal was made. I considered refusing to meet officials from the Deputy High Commission or withdrawing my agreement to return to England, but hesitated to take such drastic steps, knowing that any action of that kind would be used to malign me and would mean total disruption of my contacts with family and friends in Britain, as all my mail was sent via the Calcutta office.

I was still considering what I might usefully do to improve my situation when, on the eve of April Fool's day, 1973, I was informed that I was to be transferred to Jamshedpur next morning.

# 8. Tata

That night, Rajkumari took out the few ounces of rice she had saved, handful by handful, to sell in exchange for tobacco for her earthenware pipe, and soaked it in water. Next morning she was up long before dawn, grinding it to make my favourite *chilka*, thin rice pancakes. Balko, matine since Nago's release earlier that year, made *halva* from flour and molasses. They spread a blanket on the dormitory floor and called me to join them for a farewell breakfast. I had been with them nearly three years, day and night. Soon after eating, I was summoned to the office. There were tears in my own eyes as I saw Rajkumari and Leoni crying to see me go.

Sentimental thoughts were soon rudely shattered. Armed guards and Special Branch police awaited me at the jail gate. They searched my bags, strewing letters, clothing, sanitary cloths, across the cobbled ground in full view of office staff, convicts and the crowd of curious onlookers hanging around the jail entrance. Two women police had come all the way from Patna to accompany me. They took me into a toilet behind the Superintendent's office and searched me, roughly thrusting their hands into my underclothing. One scornfully fingered the cheap saree I was wearing, asking me why my husband had not bought me a nice one. In fact it was one I had exchanged with another prisoner for one of mine that she had liked.

Despite an escort of three police vehicles bearing seventeen armed guards, several Special Branch men, the two women police and a wardress, I was excited and elated by my first view of an open road and fields after so long behind stone walls. One of my escorts started singing, others became talkative and the driver stopped to buy pawpaw for us to eat on the way. Soon they started asking me about Amalendu, my family, and Britain. When we got round to the subject of politics, I found that, like many of the police I encountered during my subsequent journeys back and forth, they were by no means wholly unsympathetic to Naxalites.

It was night when we reached Jamshedpur, 130 miles south-east of Hazaribagh. The Jailer was expecting my arrival and was waiting for me in his poky little office. He noted down my particulars and told me to leave my khaki bags in the office over-night so that they could be searched through once more. A warder took me to my cell. It was about half the size of the one in Hazaribagh, and as sparsely furnished; it was surrounded by its own yard and wall and so was totally separated from the rest of the female section. I folded the familiar grey blankets on the stone floor and tried to sleep, my body still swaying from the un-accustomed motion of the jeep. An old wardress came to check the lock and exchanged a few friendly words with me. Eventually I fell asleep, thinking about the trial that was due to start, the Jailer had said, in two days' time.

When I awoke, it was half light. Used to estimating the time without a watch, I folded my blankets and waited for the warder to come and unlock my cell. Hours passed and it did not get any lighter. The red 'morning glow' I could see was, I afterwards discovered, from the furnace of the steel plant on the other side of town.

Both the town and the jail of Jamshedpur were a complete contrast with Hazaribagh, a quiet country spot whose relatively cool climate attracted missionaries and retired civil servants. Now I was in one of India's earliest industrial cities. The steel plant had been built not long after the turn of the century by the Tata family, still today among India's biggest industrialists. Following that, a host of other industrial establishments had sprung up in what had been a village in a tribal area. The rich mineral wealth of the region, which included copper and uranium, had attracted Indian and foreign capital, and the original inhabitants had been forced further and further back into the surrounding jungle areas as the city of Jamshedpur had grown. The town built by the Tatas still largely belonged to them and was popularly known as 'Tata'. Even the jail was situated on what had been their estates.

Jamshedpur jail was small and extremely crowded. At that time there were already 700 prisoners in buildings designed to accommodate 137. Of all the inmates, only I enjoyed the luxury of a cell to myself. The place was grossly understaffed, and, consequently, the administration in general was more haphazard even than in Hazaribagh. On the first morning, looking through the barred gate in the eight-foot high wall that separated me from the other women, I could see the small single-storeyed, square, cage-like building that housed them. There was nothing of the spaciousness of Hazaribagh. Views on all sides were of high walls. My own cell and surroundings were neat and clean, the walls newly whitewashed, and I had the unhoped-for luxury of a water tap and small concrete trough to myself. Afterwards I found out that, in the male sector, even at that time, several hundred prisoners were sharing two taps.

The women's conditions were bad enough. There were never less than thirty prisoners, and when I finally left Jamshedpur two years later, there were forty-four women and twelve children sharing the fifteen-feet square cage. At night they were packed in rows, unable to turn one way or the other without great difficulty, young and old, sick and healthy, mad and sane, all crammed in together. The single latrine had to be reached by stepping over the bodies of those who had the misfortune to be sleeping in front of it. The drain leading from it ran overground across the yard at the back, and the stench rose through the open bars on three sides.

Days were not much better than nights. Jamshedpur is notorious for its heat and humidity. Summertime temperatures reach forty-five degrees centigrade. Once the sun rose, there was hardly a shady spot in the yard. The women and children spent their days sitting or lying about amidst the smell of urine and rotting food, buzzing flies, sweating bodies, disease, sores and leaking water taps surrounded by slimy puddles. Water was conserved in a cracked concrete trough with a piece of old rag stuffed in it as a plug. There was nothing to do, nowhere to sit or eat in comfort, no bucket for washing clothes, sometimes not even enough dishes and tumblers to go round; and not a hope of peace or privacy.

My first court appearance was set for Tuesday, 3 April 1973. The afternoon before, a visitor came to my cell, a plain clothes police officer whom I recognized as being among those who had interrogated me after my arrest. He was now in charge of Naxalite cases. After some polite remarks about the amount of weight I had lost, he came to the point: my case was about to come up for trial, and the 'general idea', as he put it, was 'confession and pardon'. This would do away with unnecessary formalities and delays and ensure a speedy return to my own country. I asked him what would happen if I chose not to confess. He shrugged his shoulders and said, 'Well, you know the sentence for treason and sedition. It will mean twenty years.' I told him to act according to his principles, and I would stick to mine.

That night I lay reflecting on the implication of his words. The police had charged me together with fifty-one other people, including Kalpana and Amalendu. All were still in jail awaiting trial. The government had responded to moves made on my behalf by separating my case, but were trying to make use of my willingness to return to Britain to obtain a 'confession', which might indeed buy my personal freedom but would no doubt be used to incriminate the people who had been arrested in the same area as I. As yet I did not even know what they wanted me to 'confess' to, but in any case it was out of the question. If they could put me on trial, then why not try the others too? Some of them had been transferred at the same time as Kalpana to Calcutta; the Bengal police also wished to prefer charges against them. But there were thirty-five people left in Hazaribagh. Their position, in all essentials, was identical to mine, but, while I was to be 'tried', and maybe released, they were to remain in jail, in fetters, for goodness knows how many years to come.

After considering all these points, I decided to ask the magistrate next day to order that those of my co-defendants still in Hazaribagh also be brought to Jamshedpur for trial. Next morning, amidst the clicking of bayonets, jangling of keys and clanging of iron gates, I was whisked off in a police truck to the local courts, and ushered into the dock. The magistrate glanced up from his writing, looked at me, motioned to the police escort, and within ten minutes I was back in my cell. After nearly three years, this was my first 'court appearance'. I did not even know what date had been set for the next one. The Jailer looked at my warrant and told me it was 17 April. Before that date, however, I had a visit from Amalendu's sister and the lawyer the family had appointed for me. She said Amalendu, who had somehow heard the news of my transfer, was sure they were preparing to send me off to England without delay and had urged her to come and see me one last time. I assured her that nothing so prompt was going to happen.

I had received one more postcard from Amalendu, who was in Alipur Central Jail, but for every one that arrived there were five or six that did not. As I was unable to find any logic in the censorship imposed on me, I had once written a petition asking for clarification of what I was permitted to write. Like all prisoners' petitions, it went unanswered. No doubt it too had gone to swell the piles of waste paper in the room beneath the central watch-tower in Hazaribagh Jail. Once the Chief Head Warder there brought me some spinach wrapped in a piece of paper which, on inspection, I found to be a petition I had written for another woman a week or two before.

On 17 April I did not enter the court at all. I was driven up to it in a police truck, the magistrate came and stood on the steps to make sure I was there, then disappeared back inside the court. Fortunately, my lawyer was there and I asked him to submit a petition for my co-defendants to be brought from Hazaribagh. The magistrate promised to give his verdict a fortnight later. Meantime, a courtroom was being prepared inside the jail as the magistrate had granted the prosecution's petition to hold the hearings there. Delays in the completion of this courtroom and in bringing the others from Hazaribagh caused the start of committal proceedings to be postponed for nearly three months.

Bina introduced herself to me on my first morning in Jamshedpur, taking care to make sure that the matine did not see her talking to me. It was from Bina that I learned most of all about the lives of India's peasants, and I came to love and respect her more and more in the months that followed. About the same age as I, she came from a family of landless peasants, and from childhood had worked as a labourer in the fields of landlords of her area. She had been married as a young girl, but her father was too poor to give her much dowry and so she had been ill-treated by her husband and mother-in-law. She had too strong a will to put up with this type of behaviour and, taking her infant daughter with her, had returned to her father's house in the Bengal district of Midnapur, where, in 1970, the Naxalites had been on the point of establishing their second liberated zone.

The police who had arrested her in late 1971, accusing her of being a Naxalite, had kept her in the police station for over a week, beating her every day in the course of their interrogations, before sending her to jail in a state of semi-consciousness and covered in blood and bruises. After recovering somewhat, she was again taken off to the station for another week of interrogations and beating. Her body was still covered in scars when I met her, and the beating had somehow damaged her ears, causing her to feel dizzy sometimes and giving her headaches and frequent attacks of fever. But Bina was tough. What had disgusted her most of all was that the police had not even given her a piece of cloth to use during menstruation. Not that conditions were much better in this respect inside the jail. In Hazaribagh, a bundle of dirty, lice-ridden, cast-off clothing stinking of sweat was sometimes tossed over the gate for the women to sort out, wash and use as sanitary cloths. In Jamshedpur, there was no provision whatsoever. The women tore pieces from their sarees, or, if these were too ragged, used strips of blanket. After menstruation, the same cloths were washed, dried and kept for the next month.

When I first met Bina, her father had recently died. She had not seen any of her family since being in jail, because they were too poor to save up the ten rupees fare to Jamshedpur, plus the bribe they would have to pay at the jail gate for the privilege of seeing her. I could always tell when she was thinking about them. Every change in the weather made her pensive, considering what effect it would have on the crops, and, consequently, on her family's fortunes. If there was no work in the fields and they fell into difficulties, they had no option but to take a loan of paddy from one of the local moneylenders, who charged 100 per cent interest. Before meeting her, I had treated any freak weather or sudden storm as a welcome change from jail monotony and a relief from the intense heat, without stopping to reflect that crops could be ruined and people made destitute overnight by Nature's whims.

Bina had been right to be wary of the matine when talking to me. This woman was the only one of my fellow prisoners whom I ever really disliked. Dressed in a silk saree that had once been gaudy but was now faded and dirty, her sleek plump forearms encircled by gold bangles, her waistline wreathed in a tyre of fat that hung over the top of the saree that she always tied beneath her navel, she reminded me from the very first of a brothel-keeper. I was not far wrong. I soon heard from the other prisoners that she was a procuress, and earned large amounts of money by selling young girls to rich businessmen and farmers or into brothels in distant parts of the country. She and her four daughters, all out on bail, were only a small part of a whole network of girl traders. Their particular role was to befriend young girls from poor homes and lure them away with promises of good food, clothes and an escape from drudgery. Three of the girls she had planned to sell were in Chaibasa jail, where they were being held until the case came up in court and their statements could be taken. Whereas the procuress herself was later released on bail, the girls were still in prison when I left India two years later although there were no charges against them. Every time a prisoner was transferred to Chaibasa, the Jamshedpur matine sent a message warning them not to make any statement against her, or else to take the consequences.

As the days passed and I saw how this woman behaved towards the other prisoners, I despised her more and more. It was, even in Hazaribagh, the normal practice for the matine to search new prisoners, after which their possessions were returned to them, and any valuables deposited in the jail office. The procuress had her own methods. She used to seize upon new prisoners' few coins, tobacco, jewellery, matches, handkerchiefs, anything that she could possibly re-sell or add to her own hoard. I later learned that everything she was wearing, including her jewellery, had been obtained by threats, theft or flattery from other prisoners. She ruled the women with a rod of iron, abusing and swearing at them, hitting them, stealing and selling their rations, and, something that earned her more enmity than anything else, telling tales on them to the warders. Several times I saw women beaten by warders as a result of her malicious stories, though, in the end, after my protests, the Superintendent did order the warders not to touch female prisoners.

From the start she resented the hours that Bina and I spent together, and became so abusive towards Bina that I had to tell her not to interfere with us. That evening she told the warder that I had hit her. It was a lie of course, but as he shared in her profits, he naturally took her side and carried the whole tale to the Jailer. The gate that divided me from the other women, which, after my initial request, had been left open, was now locked again. By this time, however, I realized that in the conditions prevailing in the jail, there was little I could do except to try to get permission for Bina to spend the days with me. I told the Superintendent that I could not possibly manage the work of cleaning my cell, sweeping the yard and so on, alone, and must have a companion. I knew that this kind of talk would sound quite logical to him; he would not expect an 'educated' person to do manual work. He allowed me to have Bina as my 'attendant'. We did not care how he defined her, as long as we were together. The type of cunning that I practised quite auto-matically on this and other occasions had been something com-pletely alien to me before coming to jail; but it was a necessary weapon in the battle for survival and one which most prisoners soon acquired.

Now that we had relative peace and quiet, with the limited Bengali that I had learned, I started teaching Bina to read and write. She made rapid progress. We bought some chalks and wrote on the stone floor to save paper. I did not even know the names of all the Bengali letters, though I had an idea as to what sounds they represented, and my teaching methods were very unorthodox, but within a few months she was able to write a postcard to her mother. Not that postcards ever reached their destination. The postage entered in the records just helped to fill the clerks' and writers' pockets.

Apart from all she taught me about village life, Bina, an extremely practical person, showed me how to scour our aluminium dishes with sand until they gleamed like silver, to polish the oil lamps till they shone, to get clothes clean with hardly any soap. At night she was locked in with the other women, but we welcomed this arrangement, which allowed her to maintain contacts with the rest of the prisoners, and me to catch up on the reading I had not done during the day.

In Hazaribagh, we had heard about the riots that had shaken Jamshedpur Jail in the autumn of 1970. The rioting prisoners' three main grievances had been overcrowding, lack of water and absence of medical care. The disturbances had been quelled with promises of improvements. Instead, the leaders had been transferred to other jails and everything was as before. In the male section, up to one hundred prisoners were locked in a cell the same size as the women's, infectious diseases raged and at least one corpse was carried out nearly every day. On the other hand, one could, by bribing a warder, or a 'trusty', ensure a relatively comfortable place to sleep in and a double helping of food, which was cut from the rations of those too poor to pay and too timid to fight. The contractors' men who delivered jail supplies paid the 'trusties' in charge of checking incoming goods so that shortages in weight or inferior goods passed un-challenged. On several occasions I witnessed protests by male prisoners in both Hazaribagh and Jamshedpur about some ill-treatment or injustice. These usually took the form of climbing on to the roof or up a tree and refusing to come down until their grievance was remedied. But any resulting improvements were always shortlived and the System soon took over again.

There were no facilities in Jamshedpur for cooking one's own food, and, rather than have special arrangements made just for me, I ate the same as everyone else, but made tea, which was not generally supplied, on a small primus stove. The jail kitchen was just beyond the wall that ran in front of my cell. At about three in the morning I was often woken by the noise of the big iron drums in which our rice was cooked being rolled to the water taps. The cooks had to start early because the kitchen was equipped to cater for only about a quarter of the number of prisoners in the jail at that time, and the food had to be pre-pared in relays. By about four-thirty, the peculiar smell of un-washed rice being cooked filled the air. The boiled rice would then be tipped out on sacks spread across the verandah in front of the kitchen, where it was left, exposed to flies, birds and dust, until being served up to prisoners at ten or eleven o'clock.

The slimy rice and half-raw *chapatis* played havoc with my digestion, and within a couple of weeks of my arrival, this and the Jamshedpur heat had taken their toll. I went down with heat fever, followed by dysentery. The heat reached its peak in May. I was bathed in sweat twenty-four hours a day, and was afraid to wash my hair because it never dried, and just hung lank and clammy round the nape of my neck, causing sores. All of us had prickly heat. I felt uncomfortable and irritable most of the time. To sit and study for a couple of hours was a supreme effort; my head, heavy and muzzy, seemed to sink further and further towards the ground. Once in a horizontal position, it was hard to stand up again. The heat made my veins swell and seemed to stop my blood from flowing. My joints ached so much that my knees would hardly bend to climb the two steps up to my cell. At nights I lay nearly naked on the stone floor, thinking about the Naxalite prisoners in heavy iron fetters, and of the women and children packed together in the intolerable atmosphere of the cell just across the wall from mine. Compared to them, I was living in comfort.

Two of the Naxalite prisoners, men from the same district as Bina, went down with smallpox. Many other male prisoners were affected, but, by a miracle, the women escaped. But one thing that eventually affected every single one of us was scabies, the dreaded Itch. In the middle of the night I would wake up itching all over and would not be able to sleep again until I had indulged in a frenzy of scratching with my hairbrush. The only comfort the doctor could offer were a couple of unnamed white tablets which were of no use at all. In fact I was not finally cured until I returned to Hazaribagh that winter and was given the correct ointment. Other prisoners were not so fortunate. Many were covered in septic sores, and one day I saw a prisoner in the office whose feet were so swollen and full of poisonous matter that he could hardly walk. The Jailer told me it was useless to treat 'them' as they 'did not keep themselves clean' and the jail was overcrowded anyway. How he expected men to keep clean in those conditions without soap, water or a change of clothing, I do not know.

In mid-June my co-defendants were finally brought from Hazaribagh. A few days later, on 19 June 1973, our usual morning routine of cleaning and bathing was broken by the sound of slogans mingled with the clank of fetters and shouts of 'Hit! Kill!' We stood petrified, trying to make out what actions were accompanying the sounds, which drew nearer until they stopped right in front of my cell, on the other side of the high wall. There followed a terrifying ten minutes of shouts, cries and heavy blows. We heard a boy's voice cry, 'Water! Give me water!' Another was groaning, 'Oh, mother.' Bina and I stood, silent, looking questioningly at each other. The other women had run to the dividing gate to be nearer the scene. All of us knew one thing, they instinctively, we from the slogans that had preceded the beating: Naxalites had been the victims. It was only when the beating had finished that the alarm bell was sounded. This was done, presumably, to add weight to the jail authorities' subsequent explanation that they had been forced to resort to violence against rioting prisoners.

After the commotion had subsided, we paced restlessly up and down our tiny yard. I longed to rush out and see what was going on, but was forced to contain myself within walls that now seemed to stifle me. Little by little, the whispers of prisoners coming to our ward on various errands informed us that six prisoners had been beaten up by warders and 'trusties'. One was still lying unconscious under the mango tree by the wall. Women returning from court at two o'clock said they thought he was dead.

I felt I must take some action to punish the warders who had taken the lead in the beating, but I too was in their clutches. All I could do was to deny them the usual politeness with which I addressed them. That day when the Chief Warder came to lock me, instead of exchanging a few words, as I usually did, I ignored him and continued pacing round my cell, singing at the top of my voice.

Next day we were due to appear in the jail 'court'. The jail authorities made some feeble excuse not to produce my co-defendants. Only I was taken to an impromptu 'court' in the jail office. Our lawyers had not been idle. A sympathetic member of the jail staff had advised them of the incident, for the six men who had been beaten were among the accused in my case. The lawyers had been refused permission to meet us, but had informed the local press of what had happened. The magistrate remained absolutely silent as I lodged my protest at the whole episode. When I had finished speaking, he merely said '*Achha*' (All right), and continued with his writing.

After the hearing I was able to find out exactly what had happened. As no tea was provided in Bihar jails my co-defendants had, in Hazaribagh, been allowed to make tea at their own expense, but the Jamshedpur jailer had forbidden them to do the same there. Several of them had experimented by making tea on the oil lamp that stood on the verandah outside their cell at night. The warder on duty had reported them to the

Jailer, who, next morning, had instructed a party of warders and convicts armed with sticks to beat them up. Already in fetters, they had been handcuffed and dragged to the central courtyard so that the sounds of the beating could be heard all over the jail, as an example, presumably, to other prisoners. The boy under the tree was not dead, but unconscious. His arm was fractured, and one other had received a serious eye injury. This was why the jail authorities did not want them seen in court.

For several days after the beating, I had a terrible headache. I felt an intense loathing for Jamshedpur Jail, for the warder who came to lock me up, the Special Branch men who leered and listened to my every word whenever I went to the office, the Jailer who took my books and papers for his sons, and coveted everything brought me by visitors. Hating my dependence on them, I did without tea rather than ask for matches to light the primus stove and went without newspapers in preference to reminding the warder to give me one.

On 30 June 1973, after more than three years in jail, I saw

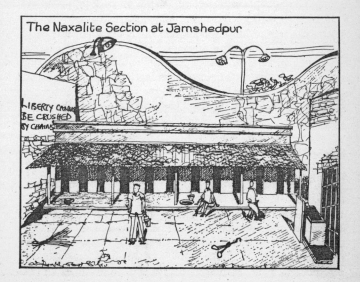

The Naxalite Section at Jamshedpur

for the first time all thirty-five of my fellow accused who had remained in Hazaribagh when Kalpana and the others went to Calcutta. It was a hot, sultry day just after the start of the monsoon season. My hands, already clammy with perspiration at six a.m., clung to my cotton saree as I tried to arrange its folds. Excited yet apprehensive at the prospect of a trial, I followed the warder through the male prisoners' quarters to the makeshift courtroom which had finally been fixed up in one of the dormitories. It was the usual long cage-like building, divided down the middle by a floor to ceiling steel mesh, on one side of which were arranged a few tables and chairs and the magistrate's bench. Overhead electric fans were whirring. The other side was completely bare, and into this I was conducted. I watched through the bars as the men filed out of their cell block just across the yard. Two by two they stood under the mango tree outside the courtroom while two 'trusties' removed their heavy iron fetters with hammers and chisels. The fetters were thrown into a heap at the foot of the tree to await their return from court, when they would be replaced before the men went back to their cells. As each pair walked into the courtroom, I had ample time to study their faces. Many of them were still not much over twenty. They walked about, taking advantage of the unique opportunity of moving unfettered. Some of them greeted me. Those with whom I had maintained secret links in Hazaribagh introduced themselves to me and I was able to put names to faces for the first time. I recognized the boy I had seen shivering in the police station after my arrest. All of them were neat and in good spirits, but I could sense an underlying nervousness. After the hearing, while their fetters were being replaced, I persuaded the warder to let me have a quick look into the block where they and other Naxalite prisoners were kept. On return to my cell, I wrote in my diary what I had seen:

The men are in dreadful conditions. Their yard is as dreary and desolate, as ugly a place as one could imagine – a cemented yard, a water tap and a row of dark little cells, in which they are locked, five or six to a cell, in fetters, twenty-four hours a day. Even in the daytime it is dark. Only if they squat in front of the barred door can they see to read. At night they do not even have a light inside their cells. And, to cap it all, one complete madman is locked up with them. Yet they laugh, joke, make light of it all. They are lively and full of spirits, but some of their faces tell a different story. Shadows under two young, bright eyes, a grey pallor beneath a brave nonchalant smile, the twitching of a facial muscle, the fidgeting of an arm or leg, show their true condition. Physically, all are affected. They are thin, pale, dry, attacked by ailments diagnosed and undiagnosed.

# 9. Committal

The committal proceedings dragged on. The police finally submitted charge-sheets and gave me a wad of documents pertaining to the case. Their account of the events leading up to my arrest, how they found me wandering in the jungle, in possession of subversive pamphlets and some acid in a plastic bottle, was pure fiction. I was charged with being part of an unlawful assembly that had thrown bombs at a police station and with being 'knowingly in possession of picric acid under such circumstances as to give rise to reasonable suspicion that the same was not for lawful object'. I had never even heard of picric acid, but I had little doubt that the magistrate would believe the police story; so far the Prosecution had had its way in almost everything, and the warning I had received of a twenty-year sentence was still in my mind.

About this time, support came from an unexpected quarter. A young warder wrote to me secretly saying that, though he was a government servant, it could not stop him from being aware of the the corruption and injustice prevailing in every government department. He was in grave doubt as to whether I would get a fair hearing and advised me to engage a barrister of the highest calibre from Patna or Calcutta if I was to have any chance of defending myself. I replied thanking him, but pointed out that I would have to be a millionairess to pay the fees of a barrister for the length of time my trial was likely to take. Actually, I was sceptical as to whether any lawyer, however brilliant, could do anything for me. I preferred to let things take their course without devoting much time to thinking about what might happen.

Ignoring the dilatory proceedings in the other half of the cage,

I used court appearances to practise my Bengali and chat with some of my co-defendants. We discussed political developments and compared experiences of the three years in Hazaribagh. Each meeting with my fellow-accused increased my respect for them; they were considerate in their behaviour towards fellow prisoners and polite, yet unflinching, with the authorities. They were always concerned to hear about my health and welfare, and to offer help in case of need. The enthusiasm I had felt in my first days in Calcutta for the zeal and spirit of self-sacrifice of the best of India's youth, and their genuine desire to work for the good of the people, was renewed.

Despite the fact that thousands of suspected Naxalites had been killed and arrested, and that we ourselves were in prison with little hope of release, I still felt that India's future lay in the hands of people like these who were honest, uncorrupted, free from old prejudices of caste and class, and able to identify with the downtrodden people who are the country's backbone.

British officials continued to visit me from time to time, but were unable to do anything to speed up the proceedings. My friends and relatives could not understand the reason for the further delays in brining me to trial. They had expected a speedy conclusion when I was taken to Jamshedpur. I was upset by the puzzled and distressed letters I received from my parents, because it was impossible to explain the real situation to them. One morning my lawyer told me that the British press had reported that I had been sentenced to life imprisonment. Concerned about the effect this report might have on my mother's health, I urged him to write to her immediately, though I had faint hopes that the letter would ever reach England; it never did.

Afterwards, I discovered that the High Commission people considered that, by requesting a joint trial with my fellow accused, I had 'refused' to be tried separately, and had thus reversed my earlier attitude. I did not consider the questions of 'voluntary repatriation' and 'separate trial' to be the same thing at all; in fact their proposal had been that charges would be withdrawn if I agreed to return to England. Taking me to Jamshedpur for a separate trial was, for me at least, an unexpected development that put a new light on the situation, particularly in view of the police's demand for a 'confession'. Even so, my petition for my co-defendants to be brought from Hazaribagh hardly amounted to a 'refusal' of any kind of trial. But, in official eyes, it all boiled down to one thing: I was being difficult. Unfortunately, this attitude proved a serious drawback to attempts being made on my behalf by friends in Britain. Every approach from any quarter to the Foreign Office met with the stock reply that I had refused a separate trial and thus spoiled my chance of an early release. They did not take the question of the false 'confession' into account at all.

A second visit from my friend Iris Marks provided me with the opportunity of giving her an explanation for the delays which, on return to England, she was able to pass on to other friends, who finally realized that it was quite likely that no trial at all would be held in the foreseeable future. They set to work to interest the press in the whole question of political prisoners in India. Though these efforts met with many obstacles and frustrations, they assured me that they would not give up; the very fact that they were trying did more to raise my spirits than any actual hope that they would meet with any success. In India too, efforts were made on our behalf. Amalendu's family had even written to Mrs Gandhi, and had received a reply assuring them that the 'necessary' would be done. That was the last anyone heard of it.

Renewed interest in our case on the part of the press was not entirely a positive development. One London daily published an article by a journalist who claimed to have spoken to me in Jamshedpur Jail but whom I in fact had never seen. The *Guardian* correspondent, Walter Schwarz, did take the trouble of coming to Jamshedpur, but was unable to obtain permission to interview me. All the same, he was able to glean sufficient information to write fairly detailed reports. Of all journalists, only he, it seemed, was able to understand my reasons for not wanting an individual trial. Many of the others concentrated on far-fetched details about my private life and my apparel. Some were openly hostile. One journalist whom I had not allowed to photograph me wrote a particularly nasty article depicting me as a ruthless advocate of terrorism. But even out of this distortion came good. An American priest in the town, learning from that article of my presence in the local jail, obtained permission to visit me. Considering my lack of potential as a convert, he was extremely kind to me and regaled me with gifts of fruit and sweets, and, most welcome of all, with loans of books from various libraries.

Gradually, conditions relaxed again and I was able to talk to the other women prisoners. Most of them, as in Hazaribagh, were 'under trial' and had little hope even of seeing a magistrate. Every fortnight or so they would be driven in a crowded old truck to the local courthouses, where the women would sit all day on the verandah, watched by the wardress, while the male prisoners were in the court lock-up, whose crowded and stifling atmosphere often made them faint. There were, however, ways out of this predicament. For three rupees, the police on guard would generally unlock a man for two hours; for five rupees they would free him for double that time. Relatives wanting to talk to prisoners would pay two rupees, and for a further consideration would be allowed to pass food to them. An unskilled labourer's average daily wages at this time were three to four rupees.

There were also ways of getting one's case settled quickly. The best bet in a minor charge was to scrape up twenty rupees to bribe the court clerk to get the case heard before the magistrate, and then, in order to avoid further delays, to plead guilty. Even if one were sentenced, it was quicker than waiting for the case to be heard by orthodox channels. One woman charged with the abduction for sale of a young girl, was able to expedite her case and was acquitted after paying out over two thousand rupees to the police officer in charge of the case, the clerk of the court and the judge himself.

One prisoner whom I liked very much was Heera, a strikingly beautiful young woman of the Santhal tribe. She was gentle, dignified and generous, smooth-skinned and broad-cheeked, tall and slender, with a natural grace and bearing that could never have been acquired by training. She never laughed, though occasionally a diffident and self-conscious smile would cross her lips. Hers was a seemingly insoluble dilemma. Without waiting for her family, who were very poor, to arrange a marriage for her, she had gone to live with a young man from her own tribe. From the start his parents had resented her, wanting a richer wife for their son, and had deliberately fixed up another marriage for him. Meantime, Heera was pregnant, and one of the neighbours kept taunting her with the fact that she was going to be thrown out of her lover's house. One day this had led to a heated argument, Heera had hit the old woman and she had died. Now Heera was in jail on a murder charge. Soon after her arrest, a son was born, but in the meanwhile the child's father had married the girl chosen by his parents. According to the custom of their village, he should have acknowledged paternity of Heera's child, but his family had paid the village council to relieve him of his responsibility. Heera's brothers wanted to help her, but were afraid to take her bail and thereby incur the displeasure of the village elders who had pronounced their sister an outcaste. If they had defied this verdict they themselves would have been ostracized, with possible loss of livelihood. They visited her occasionally and did their best within the bounds of convention to assist her but could not risk the ruin of the whole family for the sake of one member. So Heera had to be forfeited.

Another frequent visitor to my cell was Gulabi, a poor village woman of about fifty, generally addressed by the other women as 'Old Gulabi', as, by their standards, she had reached an advanced age. A few weeks before I arrived in Jamshedpur she had been hit by a warder and had fallen heavily and dislocated her shoulder. The prospects of relief from the ensuing pain in jail were nil. Her family was desperately poor and she knew it was no good expecting them to get together the money for her bail, so she was relying on her own efforts, saving up every possible coin by selling her oil and soap rations, so as to have enough for a bribe. Unfortunately, the price of settling cases was rising more rapidly than the rate at which she could possibly accumulate her few rupees, and when I eventually left Jamshedpur she had been there three years without once seeing a magistrate.

She was, like many other prisoners, completely innocent. Together with four other day labourers she had been harvesting paddy on a landlord's fields, unaware that the ownership of the particular land on which she was working was disputed by his cousin, who promptly had all the labourers, and the man who had employed them, arrested for stealing his paddy. Ironically, the two landowners settled their quarrel and Gulabi's employer was released from jail, while the labourers remained behind bars. Gulabi had been in prison for nearly three years when I left India. She saved every piece of ragged cast-off clothing she could lay hands on, somehow 'mended' it and stored it away for her granddaughter. It was just as well they were only rags. Anything wearable would never have been allowed by the matine to get as far as the jail gate.

As autumn approached and paddy harvesting time drew near again, Gulabi often talked about the money she could be earning for her family. But, even if she left jail alive, it was unlikely that she would have the strength to work in the fields again or to gather firewood in the jungle for sale in the nearby villages. With one arm incapacitated, she could not even wash her own saree, and would be just another burden for her sons.

In Hazaribagh, I had seen my first corpse. Now, in September 1973, I came the closest I had ever been to seeing a child born. Nothing I had ever imagined corresponded in the slightest with the bloody canvas that confronted me one morning just after I was unlocked. One of the women had given birth only minutes before to a baby girl. Now the mother was standing against the wall in the lean-to next to the communal cell, her clothes tucked around her waist, sweat pouring off her and blood streaming down her legs. The floor around her was covered with blood, slime and afterbirth. No wonder the Hindus considered child-birth as a dirty business fit to be handled only by women of the Chamars, one of the Harijan castes! There was nobody of that caste among the prisoners, but fortunately the matine had had the common sense to help the woman during the actual process of giving birth. Now, however, there was a general reluctance both to handle the new-born child and to help in the work of cleaning up. Bina and I set to as best we could, though we had no cleaning materials or anything to wrap the baby in. Meanwhile, the women's breakfast was being brought in by male prisoners; without so much as a glance at the woman leaning against the wall or the pools of blood lying around, they doled out the chick peas and molasses as usual and ran out. Next, the doctor arrived; being an orthodox Brahman, he was unwilling to 'defile' himself by touching either mother or child, but gave instructions to the male prisoner who accompanied him for severing and tying the cord. I am sure it was the first time in his life the poor fellow had had to perform such a task. He actually knew nothing of medicine, but, being one of the few literate prisoners, had been put in charge of the 'hospital', a small cell that had been converted into a post for handing out aspirins and other palliatives to the most seriously ill among the prisoners.

That year, the monsoon was late. The rain that should have come in June, for the paddy sowing and transplanting, now arrived in September to rot the maturing crops. All day long we would sit, confined to the cell, while the rain streamed through the leaking roof, or, if there was a wind, came in sheets and flurries through the bars. Our food was invariably late and we would wait, hungry and chilled, for hours, unable to concentrate on anything but the pangs in our stomachs. The rain forced out dozens of rats from their burrows, and the younger prisoners used to chase them, shrieking, laughing and getting covered in mud. Rat curry was considered quite a delicacy among certain of the tribal people and Harijans, and our catches were invariably cooked on improvised fires and consumed by my protein-starved companions. They urged me to sample their curry, explaining that rats are vegetarian and not at all harmful to eat. One day I managed to swallow a couple of pieces; it tasted little different from the frogs' legs I had eaten in France, or indeed from rabbit.

On those rainy days I was quite absorbed listening to Bina for hours on end, as she related stories of her past life. She told me how, in the paddy-sowing season, she had worked in the fields from dawn to dusk, bathed in the village pond and, wearing the same wet saree she had washed, returned home to cook the rice she had earned that day. Half would be eaten that night, half saved for the next morning. She would go to bed, legs itching from being submerged knee-deep in muddy water all day, hands calloused and sore, limbs aching. In the rainy season, possessing no change of clothing, she had spent much of her time soaked to the skin. This was not the tale of a single day, but a suffering and discomfort borne day after day, year after year.

From Bina I learned that all I had read before being arrested about conditions in the countryside was true. The local landlords were the only people in the villages who had sufficient stocks at all times to be able to forward loans. In her area they demanded 100 per cent interest. Government loans were sometimes made available to the Scheduled Castes and Scheduled Tribes, but these too were distributed through the village headman, who was almost invariably the landlord's nominee. He kept a large proportion of the loan stocks for himself, and replaced them at a time of year when paddy was cheaper. Those unfortunates who fell too deeply into a landlord's debt would have to work for him, perhaps for the rest of their lives, as bondsmen. Peasants who had taken loans against their next harvest would see the landlord's agent standing by to collect his share as they cut their paddy. Those who worked as sharecroppers had to provide their own implements, seeds, fertilizers and labour, and still give one-half or two-thirds of the crop to the landowner. The dependence of large sections of the rural population for their very survival on landlords and moneylenders seemed to me to make elections for the village councils or for the provincial and central governments nothing more than a formality, in which the will of those who held a strangling economic power could not fail to prevail.

1972's harvest had failed, and even as we complained and fidgeted because our food was late, two hundred million people in India that year were facing the threat of famine. Wheat had long since gone 'underground' and was available only at black market prices. The price of rice doubled within a few months. The government was insisting that there was no real shortage, but this was of little comfort to those facing the prospect of starvation. Cholera, smallpox, malaria and encephalitis broke out on a large scale, the victims being usually those unable to afford a proper diet, medicines or mosquito nets.

The Indian people, however, were not suffering in silence. The country was like a bubbling cauldron, the government like a sorcerer stirring to prevent it from boiling over but unable to quench the fire beneath. There was a food crisis, a water crisis, a fuel crisis. There were food riots in several towns of Maharashtra, strikes and sabotage in thermo-electric plants in Bihar, strikes in transport and local government, of factory workers, taxi drivers and post-office employees. Attacks on landlords' stocks of hoarded grain and on the police who came to defend them were reported in the press. There was looting of foodgrain shops in many places. In Jamshedpur itself, several dozen students were arrested after breaking into food stores and distributing the stocks to hungry people. Several times the market was closed down completely as shopkeepers protested. The newspapers were carrying almost daily reports of Naxalite activities. The Inspector Generals of Police of all the Eastern states met to discuss the movement's resurgence. The tribal people in Kankse had seized food and land from some big landowners. Rifles were seized from a police camp near Calcutta. The *Statesman* reported that the government was concerned about Naxalite infiltration into the Dhanbad colliery belt, where, it was reported, several thousand cadres had mingled with the workers in such a way as to be indistinguishable from them.

The government was also faced with increasing trouble from within its own ranks. In May that year, the Provincial Armed Constabulary in Uttar Pradesh, the biggest state, mutinied, seized the armouries in eleven towns and clashed with the army that was sent to crush the rebellion. Thirty-seven people died in the fighting. Many police fled with their weapons and, months later, had not been traced. The provincial government resigned in the aftermath of the mutiny. Bihar changed governments for

the fifth time since my arrest, due to in-fighting in the ruling
Congress Party. The Chief Minister of Gujarat resigned and
Uttar Pradesh was put under President's rule. The government
in Madhya Pradesh seemed about to topple. In Bengal, clashes
within the Congress Party itself led to twenty murders in a couple
of months.

By autumn, the country was teeming with riots for food and
coal, strikes and demonstrations, student unrest, clashes between
police and public, industrial stoppages and government splits
and resignations. The Central Government's soothings, promises
and denials, its endless parliamentary debates, were light years
removed from the people's needs. But Mrs Gandhi, on her tours
of Yugoslavia and Canada that year, was able to speak of 'non-
violence', 'humanity' and 'democracy', and to quell doubters
with assurances that soon all would be well with India. At home
again, she urged workers to surrender their right to strike in view
of the critical situation.

The September coup in Chile led the Indian Government to
utter warnings that it too was vulnerable to a similar CIA-
inspired attack. But when the United Nations voted to condemn
the junta and to instruct it to release political prisoners, India
abstained.

Beyond the mango trees that stood on the other side of my
wall lay a row of cells, one of which was inhabited by a mysterious prisoner whose name was mentioned by inmates and staff
alike only in whispers. Every evening at about nine o'clock I
heard him, his brother and nephew singing prayers before eating. All their food was sent from their home in the town. The
mystery man spent the whole day sitting in the jail office chewing
betel leaves and smoking marijuana, frequently calling, in a
commanding drawl, for tea or coke to be fetched from a nearby
teastall. A rugged and fearsome-looking character, he wore on
his forehead the vermilion mark of a devout Hindu. Little by
little I found out something about him. He owned a good deal of
property in the town and was a well-known businessman. On
the surface, he was a stalwart of the Hindu faith. At that very

time a new temple was being built in the town at his expense. However, there was another side to his character. In a mode reminiscent of the Mafia, he commanded a gang of toughs who, at his behest, would perform acts of vendetta, intimidation or robbery. With his sanction and backing, it seemed, any crime could be committed with impunity. The only reason he was in jail was that one of his rivals had threatened to kill him in revenge for a previous murder, and the magistrate was afraid to grant him bail. The jail staff went in fear of him, afraid that to incur his displeasure would put their own lives in danger. He was never locked up until long after the rest of us, and it was even rumoured that he sometimes left the jail at nights. A surprising proportion of the women prisoners knew him personally; some were indebted to him, others merely afraid of him. Tales were told of the unorthodox way in which he had made his fortune, of the pools of blood he had left behind on his road to power. It was not until two years later that I found out that the government had given him the contract for the jail supplies.

The underlying insecurity of life in jail continued. On 10 October 1973, I wrote in my diary:

Yesterday the fire was smashed, all fire-making materials seized, the ward patrolled and searched, all the little 'illegal' pastimes without which life here would be unbearable have been stopped – for the time being. After a period of strict supervision, the Lull will overcome the jail again, the administration will sink back into its sleep, fires will spark once more, tea be boiled, chick peas roasted, stale *chapatis* reheated, rice puffed in hot sand and we shall live again, for some months, with all these comforts. Yesterday's was an act of revenge, but also, I detected, of fear. For a month, despite repeated pleas, we have received no soap. Yesterday, almost unanimously, the women went on a protest hunger strike. The authorities, on seeing prisoners' unity, always panic and do their best to smash it. So they broke the mud hearth, took away twigs, paper and even dry leaves, hoping that the women would quarrel among themselves and blame each other for the loss of these 'privileges'. I tried, not entirely successfully, to persuade the women not to respond to these tactics. But, one thing is certain. We shall now get our soap. And, little by little, we shall invent and improvise until they come to uproot and destroy everything again.

Despite such incidents, the beautiful Indian autumn, as always, stimulated my imagination. I started thinking once again about what to paint, write, embroider. The air was sweet, the days elusive, shortened further by sunrise-delaying, sunset-hastening walls. Already by two-thirty the shadows were all around; columned shadows of pawpaw trees, angular shadows of grey walls, feathery shadows of mango leaves, parallel shadows of iron bars. Shadows, blue sky, a gentler sun, and, for brief moments, peace.

Just when I was beginning to enjoy the Jamshedpur climate, our committal proceedings were completed. Less than a dozen court appearances had taken seven months. No witness had identified me, no statement had been given against me. Nevertheless, I and the others were committed for trial on all charges. Now, according to 'normal' procedure, it would take another four or five years for the case to come up for trial in the Court of Sessions. It was one of the prosecution lawyers himself who urged me to write to the High Commission. He said a letter from them to the Indian Government would suffice to expedite the trial. I had my doubts, but wrote both to Calcutta and to family and friends urging them to press the Indian authorities for an early trial.

A few days later, we were transferred back to Hazaribagh to await the next summons.

# 10. Crisis

It was night when I arrived in Hazaribagh. As I passed the dormitory, figures rose to greet me in the darkness, hands stretched out through the bars to touch and welcome me. '*Salaam Eleikom, didi,*' from one of the Muslim prisoners, '*Namaste, didi,*' from Prokash's crippled mother, a handshake from Balko. Three blankets were found for me to spread in my former cell, now bare and unoccupied. The wardresses soon came with hot *chapatis* and tea made by Balko on a fire of cow-dung cakes she had thoughtfully hidden in the dormitory that evening, knowing that I might arrive cold and hungry. They had been told some days previously that I might be returning.

Next morning there was a reunion with old friends and introductions to the new arrivals. Before my rations arrived from the stores I had eaten three breakfasts. It was like coming home. I was sorry to have left Bina, I knew that Hazaribagh was a shift away from a trial, that it would be more difficult for visitors to come from Calcutta, that I would once more be isolated from my co-defendants; yet all these disadvantages faded temporarily into the warmth and pleasure I felt at seeing my former companions again. I knew that, whatever difficulties might be put in my way by the authorities, I would want for nothing that my fellow prisoners could provide.

A few women had been released, several new ones had arrived, but in seven months there had been little overall change. After four years in prison, Rajkumari had been tried and acquitted of murder in my absence, but had been sentenced to six months for brewing country liquor. She would not be released until she had served the additional time.

Winter vegetables were sprouting, the earth was fresh and the sky clear. Once more I could see the sunrise and sunset and, if I climbed up on the bars, a landscape, trees, a village, a road far beyond our walls. At last I was able to get some perspective for painting with the water colours Iris had brought me back in July. But, try as I might, I could never re-create the early morning light, the first sunray falling on the corner of the two-storey sand-coloured building in the male sector, the blackish green of the trees, the ominous grey of walls and the brick-red earth. In contrast with the industrial haze that hung over Jamshedpur, the sky here was so clear, all outlines so sharply defined, that the watchtowers in the outer wall seemed near enough to touch. Hazaribagh glowed: sometimes the whole expanse of red earth turned to lilac, mauve, purple and gold in the light of the setting sun, and I felt as if I would burst with longing to consume and conserve those few moments that would never return. But I could never put it on paper.

More and more during the course of imprisonment I felt the need for beauty. I would sit for long minutes gazing at a single marigold that had somehow survived the Superintendent's rampages, and stuck every picture I could find on my cell walls, oblivious of artistic value, just for the sake of the colours. When my friends heard of this they sent books of paintings to me; but something they could not do was to satisfy my longing to hear the music I had loved. Sometimes in the afternoons a prisoner in the ward next door used to play sweet and plaintive melodies on his flute. He could not know that he had an appreciative listener on the other side of the wall.

The very size of Hazaribagh Jail reduced the tension in the atmosphere. We could not, as in Jamshedpur, hear what was going on in the male sector, the clanking of fetters, the shouts and blows. But I no longer harboured any illusions. The fact that things were out of sight and earshot did not mean that they did not exist.

One of the prisoners most glad to see me was Moti, a slightly mad Santhal woman whom I had first seen in Jamshedpur. She was gentle, reasonable and extremely hardworking until something upset her, whereupon she went off into one of her fits of rage. Somehow, she adopted me as her *beti*, or daughter, and as the wardresses were rather afraid of her outbursts, they often called to me to reason with her, though I was usually no more successful than they. Sometimes after being quiet all day she would, on being locked alone in the tiny dark cell diagonally opposite mine, remember something that had displeased her during the day, and ruin everyone's sleep by shouting terrible curses on everyone she could think of, rattling her bars and demanding to be let out, 'What do you think I am?' she would shout. 'A goat? Don't you think I'm human, locking up like this? I'm going home. Come and let me out! Come on! Come on! COME ON!' She would tuck her saree up round her waist in preparation for a fight with anyone who came near her.

One morning she started shouting at about three o'clock and it took us some time to realize that this was because she had diarrhoea and was upset by the stench from her tub. When the warder eventually came to open her cell at six o'clock as usual, without even waiting for him to go away, she dashed out carrying the tub to empty it. Unfortunately she tripped and hurled the whole lot across her verandah in front of the Chief Head Warder, splashing him with nightsoil. We were unable to suppress our laughter. Even the wardresses were smirking behind their sarees. The Warder was at once too disgusted and astonished to say anything.

Moti was an enormous eater, and always hungry. That winter, with the increasing food crisis, jail rations had diminished further than ever, and the prisoners had not eaten any flour for months. We were only given a few handfuls of rice to cook each day. Unlike wheat, rice is very quickly digested and one soon feels hungry again after eating it, particularly in cold weather. The other prisoners somehow disciplined themselves and even continued saving a little rice to sell. This made Moti furious. She wanted to save money like the others, but on the other hand, quite understandably, she wanted to eat her fill as well. In jail conditions, the two were incompatible. Luckily she had an incredibly strong digestion. Every day she searched the garden for leaves: pea, chilli, tomato, potato, onion and garlic leaves –

nothing edible was rejected. These she 'cooked' in her aluminium dish on the dying embers of our fire. This half-raw and stinking mess she then proceeded to swallow in huge mouthfuls, without stopping to chew it. She was always willing to share what she cooked, but somehow the rest of us were never able to relish this delicacy as much as she did.

One of the new prisoners was a deaf and dumb girl of about sixteen. Nobody knew her name or why she was there, except that the police had picked her up in a town about thirty miles away and sent her to jail. When I left Hazaribagh in 1975, she, like many of the others, was still there. Unable to talk or reminisce, as the rest of us did, about her past life, her home and family, she suffered mental agonies that were evident from her unbalanced behaviour. Sometimes she consumed several days' rations at one meal, not even bothering to wait until the rice was properly cooked. On other occasions she would sleep for several days, eating nothing at all. Neither she, Moti, nor any other mentally sick prisoners received any treatment apart from an occasional injection to quieten them down if they got too wild. Jail was hardly the place for them; their presence put increased stress on the other prisoners, the wardresses were not trained to cope with them and the authorities did not care as long as they were locked up out of sight during inspections. Every mentally disturbed person I saw come to jail grew gradually more insane. The doctors could do little except urge their transfer to a mental home, but this was rarely granted, for there were very few facilities. There were, a jail doctor told me, over eighty lunatics in the male section at Hazaribagh.

Just as badly off as the mentally sick were the 'safe custody' prisoners. Shortly before Christmas 1973, Satya, a girl of about eleven, wearing a ragged saree, was brought into the female ward. Her parents were tea plantation labourers in Assam and she and her father, who was carrying some money he had saved, had been on their way to visit her sick grandmother in a Bihar village, when at a railway station some men had called him away. That was the last she had seen of him. She was picked up by police some days later and sent to jail for 'safe keeping'. Unfortunately, that was the end of it. Nobody bothered to trace her family or do anything about sending her home. When one of the Christian wardresses offered to look after her, the Assistant Jailers and the Clerk of the Court warned Satya against it: Christians ate beef and she would lose caste. Instead, she was left to grow up in jail.

As the weather got colder, I began to indulge in idle thoughts of a hot bath and of sleeping on a soft bed in a warm room. But life's immediate problems were too pressing for daydreaming of any kind. There were usually at least one or two prisoners ill, and most of the women were in indifferent health all the time. Many had symptoms of liver and kidney trouble, and nearly all suffered from body pains of one type or another, some caused, no doubt, by sleeping on the cold stone floor. Anaemia was almost universal. Intestinal parasites caused lassitude and nausea. Boils, sores and other symptoms of malnutrition or vitamin deficiency were so commonplace that one almost ceased to notice them. The women themselves were so used to ill health from an early age that they shrugged off their troubles with a '*Kya korega?*' (What can you do?) until they were really unable to stand up. One reason for the predominance of under-nourishment in females was that in many families protein foods were reserved for the consumption of males.

Compared with my companions, I was a giantess. In all my five years in jail I met only a couple of women taller than myself, though I am only five feet two, and a few, usually members of the middle class, who were heavier than I, though my weight dropped to just over eight stone. Some women weighed only about five stone, yet it was nothing to see them carry heavy buckets of water on their heads or work all day carrying earth from one part of the garden to another.

Hardly any of the women had seen a doctor before coming to jail. The jail doctors, like the rest of the staff, were merely doing a job and trying to get what they could out of it. Some had become totally unresponsive to the misery around them, others tried to relieve it by indiscriminately prescribing worm medicine or pain killers. Both attitudes were equally ineffective as far as the prisoners' general health was concerned. Often I had the impression that the jail was a testing ground for new drug lines, because it was rare for the same tablets to be prescribed twice for the same complaint.

The food situation continued to deteriorate. An increasing number of items had become unobtainable, though most were available on the black market. In jail things were going from bad to worse. At one stage even the morning chick peas disappeared and were replaced by a couple of spoonsful of slimy rice cooked with a little molasses. This concoction was made from all the broken rice left at the bottom of sacks and was full of straw and husks. Most of the rice we were given that year tasted musty, as if it had been stored for a long time. The daily vegetable continued to vary between worm-eaten aubergine and cauliflower leaves and stalks, dished out as carefully as caviar. The lentils served up twice a day were ancient, worm-ridden and bitter. When the chick peas reappeared, they too were little more than skins perforated by the holes of maggots that had eaten away the centre. On the occasions when potatoes were served, they were not much bigger than peas, and black with disease. The women's discontent grew, but, as adversity increased, there seemed to be fewer quarrels among them, and the matine herself was no longer so willing to work for the authorities, since most of the perks she had enjoyed had been withdrawn.

One section of the prison population, however, was prospering from the crisis. The mates in charge of various stores and the writers in the jail office had wormed their way further into the confidence of the Chief Head Warder, whose monthly income from bribes and other illegal sources was reputed to be between six and seven thousand rupees. It was said that he had managed to buy himself several taxis and thirty acres of land on a salary which even then stood at little over three hundred rupees a month, hardly sufficient to feed his family. Under his patronage, the mates ran profitable businesses, selling food, clothing and other supplies intended for the prisoners, and paying him a portion of their proceeds each month. I was interested to note how the English word 'income' had been adopted in Hindi to mean illicit income over and above one's regular earnings. The mates had separate cells and their own servants among the prisoners; some of them kept young boy prisoners who attracted them. They ate sumptuously and wore expensive clothes laundered for them by the prison washermen. They sent home regular money orders and one was rumoured to have had a house built to await his release. They were the lords of the jail and were hated by the rest of the inmates.

Those I personally despised most of all were the mates in charge of medical supplies and hospital food. It was only when a prisoner was seriously ill that any special diet or medicines were prescribed at all, and I felt nothing but contempt for people who suffered no pangs of conscience as they grew fatter and sleeker on the proceeds of selling food and medicaments meant for sick men, women and children. None of this could have taken place without the approval of the Chief Head Warder, and the higher echelons of jail staff, though aware of what was going on, preferred not to intervene. The Jailer himself was known to receive regular payments from the mates, and the office staff had first choice of any supplies that arrived from outside. Local dignitaries and 'inspectors' who visited the jail left laden with gifts, and the Superintendent entertained with an extravagance that was widely talked about. When his daughter was married, prisoners in the tailoring workshop were put to work for many days making cushions and other items for the comfort of the guests. All the jail staff used the prisoners as their personal servants. Each morning and afternoon, groups of prisoners went to their homes to fetch water, wash clothes, cook, clean, mend or do anything else that needed doing, including massaging them.

Corruption did not stop with the Jail Superintendent. One superintendent told me that he hated the periodic visits made by Ministers or other high officials. When I asked why, he replied: 'They always ask me for money. And if I don't give it to them they will arrange my transfer to some remote jail miles and miles away, where there is no social life and I can never see my family. If I want to stay here, I have to pay up.' The jail staff, of course, had their favourite postings. There was keen competition to be transferred to industrialized towns like Jamshedpur and Dhanbad, where prisoners had more money than in country places like Hazaribagh, and where, too, relatives could be expected to pay handsomely to visit somebody in jail, or to make sure that a prisoner was well-treated.

In contrast with the mates, those prisoners who had saved a little money by selling their own rations were always in danger of losing it. Warders would ask prisoners for money and if they refused to pay up would threaten to report them to the Jailer for some alleged offence. It would be their word against a warder's, and they usually paid the required amount to avoid punishment. Several times I saw prisoners running up to the Chief Head Warder to thrust notes into his hand. The usual approach towards somebody he thought was not giving him enough would be to say, 'Well, so-and-so, you haven't treated me lately, I suppose you fancy a spell of solitary, eh?' Once there was a rumour that the Chief Head Warder was going to be transferred to Patna Jail, and I jokingly congratulated him, telling him that he would meet all the 'top people' there in the state capital. His reply was unhesitating: 'What do I want with the top people? It's the poor I get my money from.'

On days when the Minister for Jails, the Inspector General for Prisons or some other exalted personage was due to come and inspect us, we were chivvied from the time we were unlocked until they had finally departed. Those days were the only times when our latrines received any proper disinfectant; the gutters were limed to make them look presentable and hide the cracks, everything had to be cleaned and all our possessions hidden in our blanket rolls, as if it would offend their eyes to see our shabby clothing and the other miserable objects that we cherished. We were not even allowed to cook our food until they had gone. Prisoners were warned not to mention their difficulties to the visiting dignitary. Fear of reprisals usually made them comply, though occasionally one of the bolder women would step forward out of the line of prisoners standing to attention and complain about the food, lack of clothing or her long detention without trial. The visitor would say, 'All right, all right, I'll see to it.' That would be the last she heard of it. The retinue of officials and jail staff would snigger among themselves at the woman's country accent or ragged appearance, and often address snooty comments in English to each other. Then the Superintendent would make what he thought was a witty remark like, 'Well, we'd better get out, these women are dangerous types, you know, murderesses and all that, they might decide to bump us off.' Then the whole train would depart, without so much as a hint of regret at the women's deplorable conditions. The women themselves resented the Superintendent's showing off to his cronies and the treatment of prisoners as objects of amusement and ridicule perhaps more than anything else they had to put up with. Furthermore, whenever one of these visitors came, every flower that had survived in our garden was plucked to make garlands for him. That winter I tried to keep a flower bed but gave up when I saw all the blooms being carried off to grace the necks of various dignitaries or the Superintendent's house.

The only time, I think, that a visit from a high official had any practical outcome as far as we were concerned was in January 1974, when our water tap was mended. Workmen had come weeks before to replace the old cracked pipes, but all they had done was to wrench the tap out, leaving a hole in the wall through which water alternately gushed and trickled at unpredictable intervals. One never knew if any bathing operation, once begun, could be completed before the water stopped flowing. It was nothing unusual to be left with hair, body or clothes caked in soap, unable to rinse them until the water started trickling through the hole again. Even after the tap was replaced, our troubles were not over. Our water supply was connected with that of the male ward next door, and every time the prisoners there turned their tap on, ours went off. The sheer frustration of trying to get water out of a tap controlled by invisible hands made us bad-tempered and argumentative. There were always at least thirty women and children sharing this one tap; one person would be bathing, another washing clothes, a third wanting water for drinking and cooking, while someone else was try-

Inside the Female Ward

ing to fill a bucket to wash the floor or water the garden. The men next door had a well, but the rope had long since broken and not been replaced, so we could hardly blame them. But sometimes it was all so infuriating that the women began hurling insults at them. One day a couple of the younger women started throwing stones and clods of earth over the wall, and were severely reprimanded by the warder on duty next door.

I urged the wardresses to report the water problem to the Jailer, but they never did so. The conditions in their own living quarters were, if anything, even worse than inside the prison itself. Each family's accommodation consisted of a small, low room and a tiny verandah and courtyard. Up to eight or nine people might be living in this confined space. Leoni actually preferred being on duty in our ward to staying at home in her small dark quarters, teeming with flies and mosquitoes, and stinking from the open gutter that ran along the alley outside.

One day that winter one of the wardresses returning from taking a prisoner to court told us how she had seen a young girl, dressed only in a filthy loincloth, writhing with hunger on the ground outside the court. She confessed that she had not known what to do; she was too poor to feed another mouth permanently, and giving the child food for just one day was useless, it would only postpone her death until tomorrow. The wardress's description left me feeling sad, guilty, and angry. Meantime, in Delhi, the parliamentary debates continued as to whether deaths occurring in several states were from starvation or malnutrition. Every time famine struck, the same inane discussion was repeated, as if there were any fundamental difference between the two, as if deaths from malnutrition were acceptable, because starvation had been averted!

At the beginning of January 1974, the inevitable happened. Hunger protests began in Gujarat. The army was sent to control demonstrators, curfew was imposed in seventy-three towns, there were daily reports of police firings, and, by the beginning of February, government officials were admitting that forty people had been killed by police bullets. In Bihar, too, unrest was on the increase. A general strike was called for 21 January. A warder, who had just returned from Dhanbad, told me there were police wearing gas masks stationed every few paces, as the people were in a state of revolt due to food shortages.

On Republic Day, 26 January, the President, V. V. Giri, appealed to the nation for discipline. I wondered what they were to discipline – their hunger pangs, maybe? Their crying children? Their wrath against a government that offered them speeches instead of food? Mrs Gandhi may have been right in saying that there was no food shortage, but the food was not reaching the people; they had no money to buy it at the prices being demanded, and, when they went to loot it from the hoards of big farmers and merchants, they were shot. In Gujarat, riots continued in the towns of Ahmedabad, Surat and Baroda. On 21 February 1974, the Hindi paper *Aryabort* reported a new record created in Independent India: police had fired in thirty-four places in a single day, killing at least five people and injuring many others. It was the first time since 1947 that so many separate police firings had taken place on one day.

The winter continued cold and dry. Huddling at night round

the warm spot of our smuggled fire, I listened to my cellmates' recollections of the great famine of 1966, and was compelled to reflect yet again on how little I really knew of life's hardships. They had lived and brought up children through famine, trudged endless miles in search of their next meal, broken stones and lifted earth to build roads in return for a single bowl of *khichri*. Little wonder that they were worrying about their families now that widespread famine was threatening again.

In February a child was brought into our care. Her father, a widowed coalminer, had gone on hunger strike outside the colliery manager's office after being made redundant. On the fifth day he had been arrested, and since there was nobody to look after his three-year-old daughter, he had been obliged to bring her to jail with him. The Chief Head Warder had insisted that she be kept in the female ward. It was a revelation to see the condition of this worker's child. Her belly was distended through eating a diet that consisted almost solely of starch. Her hair was matted and full of lice because they were unable to afford oil or soap or to get sufficient water. Her body was covered in blisters. We fed her, cut her hair, deloused and bathed her. One of the women brought her a new dress. Fortunately her father's colleagues soon took bail for him; but the few days of her stay had been another poignant reminder of the plight of people outside.

Once, while I was in Jamshedpur, Leoni had fallen asleep on night duty. Of his own accord, the Chief Head Warder had intervened with the Jailer to save her from possible suspension. Now I noticed that for several days she had been very depressed. One afternoon as we sat sewing together, I asked her what the matter was. To my surprise, she started crying. Wiping away the tears, she said the Warder had been reminding her that she had not yet paid him for saving her job. What he wanted was not money; he wanted to sleep with her. One day he had stopped her husband in the street and told him to send his wife along that afternoon. Understandably sickened by his pursuit, she had refused to go. Now every time she came on duty or left for home, when she could not avoid seeing him, he threatened that he would get her sacked if she did not oblige him. She was determined not to succumb to this intimidation, but, knowing the extent of his influence in the jail, she realized that he really could have her dismissed. She was worried about what would become of her family if that happened.

The Chief Head Warder's attitude to Leoni was typical of the ill-disguised contempt that the more traditionalist of the Brahman warders had for the tribal wardresses. Their own wives were safely shut up at home and they seemed to have the idea that women who worked for their living had lost their chastity. I was often annoyed by their lewd remarks and insinuations to the younger wardresses. I had heard that high-caste Hindu men often regarded tribal and Harijan women, whom they would never have considered marrying, as their legitimate playthings, and this was borne out by everything I saw in jail.

The caste system operated in other ways among the jail staff. Although by law a certain proportion of the staff was recruited from the Scheduled Tribes and Castes, the majority of the warders, and nearly all the office staff, were Brahmans or Rajputs. The tribal and Harijan warders were nearly always given the more difficult and unpleasant postings within the jail, whereas the so-called 'high-caste' Hindus made sure that they were in charge of the hospital, the stores, the dairy and all the places where most profit was to be had.

At the beginning of March, a High Commission secretary came with a copy of a letter from my lawyer; the original had been sent to me, though I had not received it. He wrote that the case was about to come up for trial and that I should make arrangements with other people in the case for my defence. However, before I could take any concrete steps, Bihar was in uproar. All available police were posted to enforce law and order; there were none spare to escort prisoners to court or to other jails. Court appearances and transfers were stopped till further notice. In fact, some days later, the courts themselves ceased to function. The Bihar Secretariat was put out of action by demonstrators who surrounded it, preventing officials from entering or leaving. The agitation was spearheaded by students protesting about high prices, unemployment and corruption, and demanding reforms in the educational system.

There were other excuses ready to hand to prevent our trial from starting; a smallpox epidemic was raging in Jamshedpur and had affected the jail; the authorities there had declared themselves unable to accommodate us and had asked for the trial to be held elsewhere; the Judge had refused to conduct the trial inside jail, saying the improvised courtroom was not up to standard; the Inspector General had ordered the entire Jamshedpur Jail staff to be transferred as they had also been affected by the scabies epidemic.

As the agitation outside gathered momentum, the wardresses brought news that markets had closed, transport and other services come to a halt, and that Hazaribagh, the town for the prosperous retired, had joined the ranks of the demonstrators. People were living with bated breath; each day there were whispered rumours of the latest hot news. At the first hint of trouble the armed and steel-helmeted police swarmed all over the town. A breath of wind, a crane's wingbeat, a drum, a muffled slogan, seemed to tell us what was going on outside the sterile monotony of jail. A warder's whistle, a shout or a loud noise was enough to send my nerves racing, wondering if that indefinable something which I was waiting for had happened. It was said that hundreds of demonstrators had been arrested in Patna. In Gujarat, the government had resigned in response to the people's demand. It seemed as if life would never return to normal again.

We had no brooms, no flykiller, no disinfectant, very often no water. The summer winds dried even the ink in my pen. At nights I lay by the bars, feeling the little cool breezes run across my burning flesh and longing to sleep out of doors, or anywhere but in my oven-like cell. The walls retained the sun's heat, the bars were too hot to touch, the stone floor itself was warm where the sun's rays had rested on it. I forced myself to wake long before dawn so as to have a couple of hours' quiet before the others woke. I felt the need to be alone and to think about what was happening. A cellmate's waking left me feeling almost violated, as if she had no right to break in on my private silence.

Sometimes I thought of Amalendu. I had had no news from him and little from anyone else in the months of disruption since my return from Jamshedpur.

There had been no rain for six months; it was with a certain cynicism that I read in one of the few issues of *The Times* that got through to me that year of Suffolk's being declared a drought zone after two rainless months. I wondered what would happen in Britain if the rivers, wells, ponds, streams and every water source dried up, as they had in some districts of Bihar.

That Easter was spent in the company of seven college students, the first women to be arrested in Hazaribagh in the course of the anti-government agitation. They were lively and militant, but their stay was shortlived. They were daughters of respected middle-class families and were soon granted bail. They left with promises to visit me, but I knew that it would never be allowed.

At the beginning of May, the British Consul newly put in charge of my case came to tell me that he was going to England on leave, and would try to contact my parents. I was grateful; none of those who had gone on leave before him had done so. I had been keeping two paintings for my mother, which he agreed to give to her. The Special Branch inspector took them for 'examination', promising to post them on afterwards. This was never done.

The Consul confirmed that, due to 'overcrowding and small-pox' in Jamshedpur Jail, our trial had been postponed indefinitely. He also mentioned that friends in England, headed by Jill Dimmock and Ruth Forster, had formed a committee to agitate for my release. It was the best news I had heard for months.

# 11.   The Movement

As Bihar's long hot summer continued, the newspapers became almost monotonously sensational. The daily reports of riots, strikes, demonstrations, police firing, disease, epidemics and famine that filled the Patna papers became so commonplace that one had the impression that one was reading the same issue every day. The railway workers' strike in May 1974 marked a new stage in the Central Government's methods of dealing with opposition. A week before the strike was due to start, at a time when negotiations were actually taking place between the government and the union, the railwaymen's leaders were unexpectedly arrested in pre-dawn raids on their homes and held incommunicado for several weeks. Whether the government seriously expected this action to prevent the strike I do not know; anyway it had the opposite effect. The strike began as scheduled and continued for twenty days, by the end of which time fifty thousand railwaymen were in prison, police had fired on picketers and the wives and families of railway workers had been attacked, harassed and thrown out of their living quarters. When the strike was eventually broken, after the army had been called in to run trains, those workers who had remained 'loyal' to the government were rewarded with bonus payments and members of their families were appointed to replace those who had been arrested and fired.

Night and morning, Hazaribagh Jail resounded with the railwaymen's slogans. Throughout the month of May, arrests of strikers, students, lawyers, teachers and other intellectuals under the Maintenance of Internal Security Act and the Defence of India Rules continued. As the jail filled up, supplies became more and more hazardous and the few convicts who had to do all the work looked thinner and wearier than ever. They said they had to work so hard that they did not have time to eat, bath, or sleep for more than a couple of hours each night. In Patna, the State Government performed a reshuffle in an attempt to control the explosive situation, but it was like moving the pieces round on a chess board; there was no fundamental change.

By early June we had been joined by two women détenues, a professor and a headmistress. Though at first reluctant to talk to me as she had the idea that Naxalites were preachers of violence, the professor afterwards grew quite fond of me. She told me that she had taken a delegation of her students to Delhi to meet the Prime Minister, in order to explain to her about the impossible situation in Bihar, where people were suffering near-starvation while rice and wheat were being hoarded by big merchants and farmers. After several days' wait Mrs Gandhi agreed to meet them. On hearing their description of the situation and their request that something be done about it she had replied that she thought the reports of poverty were exaggerated. Everywhere she went to address meetings she saw crowds of people wearing new clothes and carrying transistor radios.

It was after receiving this rebuff that my professor friend and her students went to Patna to take part in the great demonstration of 14 May that marked the real beginning of the *andolon*, the 'Movement' that became a byword throughout Bihar and continued unabated for the rest of the year despite all attempts to put an end to it. She described to me how on that day students squatting outside the Secretariat had been run down by police jeeps, and the blood of peaceful demonstrators had stained the streets of Patna.

The second female détenue was a member of the Jain community, a scrupulous respecter of all animal life. She walked looking at the ground for fear of trampling on an insect and killing it. Whenever she came into our cell, I could sense her distaste and discomfort as she noted the corpses of massacred flies that littered the floor. She refused to have her wooden cot sprayed with insecticide, preferring to endure the ravages of the bugs that crawled out of its crevices at night. She was from a wealthy family and had never had to combat such difficulties at home; perhaps that is how she had managed to remain faithful to her religion.

I tried to analyse the motives that had made these comparatively wealthy middle-class women join the anti-government movement. Though friendly towards the other prisoners, they retained the old contempt for manual work and the idea that the poor and illiterate were there to serve and obey them; and, unlike Kalpana or Bina, would not have considered it their responsibility to involve themselves in the other women's problems. They would not even have thought of imparting some of their knowledge to the women around them. I noticed that they often spoke of India's glorious past, and concluded that in essence they were patriots who hated to see India a country without prestige, a beggar on the international scene and ridden with corruption. They had taken part in movements to dehoard the stocks of local merchants, finding it shameful that people could be starving while food was available. For their actions they were in prison, charged with inciting the populace to rebellion. They were just two of the thousands arrested in Bihar that summer, and, like most of the others, were released on appeal to the High Court. The professor was re-arrested three times in the months that followed.

Apart from her company, which I enjoyed despite our differences, her stay had other advantages. She spent many hours in the office chatting with her students, also back in jail, and with the office staff, and used to relay all she heard there to me. Of particular interest to me was the warning that the Special Branch men had given her not to associate with me or tell me anything; they had said I was dangerous and had been arrested carrying a pistol and revolver. More important and relevant to my immediate situation, the Assistant Jailer who handled all the mail, a morose and malicious person, told her that he ripped up and threw away many of my letters. I knew of course that many letters written to and by me were not delivered, but had never been quite sure of their fate before that.

That summer the nearby Reformatory School, long since

closed, was reopened to accommodate détenus, and renamed 'Hazaribagh Special Jail'. There seemed to be no limit to the number of people ready to join the Movement, and arrests continued. My feelings about the agitation were mixed; the participants' demands were just, yet I had the feeling that many of them had joined the Movement because the middle class themselves were suffering, due to the unprecedented leap in the cost of living and the aggravating shortages of a whole range of items, from soap to sugar. I doubted, if their own immediate demands were fulfilled, whether they would continue the struggle for the large numbers of people who had been at starvation level even before the latest intensification of the crisis. Even in jail, while they agitated militantly for improvements in their own conditions, many of them were apparently oblivious of the far worse situation of most other prisoners.

Not surprisingly, the other women prisoners were somewhat cynical about the 'Movement wallahs', as they called them. These people came, wave after wave, raised demands for good food and clothing and then, after a few weeks at the most, left, taking with them anything they had been able to get out of the authorities. Other prisoners often said to me that these people would never do anything for the poor; I felt that to voice open criticism would be wrong, but made it clear that I doubted whether a spontaneous agitation of that kind, without a clear political line, could ultimately provide a solution for India. However, in the course of the Movement, many of the student participants became increasingly politicized and militant. Their sympathy helped to bring about the removal of fetters from Naxalite prisoners that summer; they shouted slogans and made representations to the jail authorities in support of the Naxalite prisoners' own hunger strike. The victory was shortlived. In the prevailing situation it was inevitable that security would be increased rather than relaxed, and, sure enough, the fetters were replaced within a fortnight, after an escape attempt at Muzaffarpur Jail, a couple of hundred miles away.

Outside, police and army contingents were too busy dealing with the daily disturbances all over the state to concentrate as much attention as usual on Naxalites. One day the front-page headlines of our daily paper were smeared with black censor's ink; but the heavy indentations of the two-inch letters enabled me to decipher the words: GOVERNMENT UNABLE TO MEET NAXALITE CHALLENGE IN BHOJPUR. Within a couple of weeks, further reports followed; Naxalites had entrenched themselves and had won considerable support among the Harijans and landless peasants of Bhojpur District in Western Bihar. It was said that students of the Movement were working closely with the Naxalites.

On 6 June there was to be a big demonstration in Patna. The day before, the paramilitary forces that had been posted there to keep the situation under control paraded through the city, as if to warn the populace that they were prepared for confrontation. Roads to Patna were blockaded, trains stopped and ferryboats impounded. Many people had entered the city several days previously in anticipation of the measures; others walked many miles to attend the demonstration. Despite all precautions, one hundred thousand people registered their protest against the government that day and demanded the resignation of the State Government and the dissolution of the Legislative Assembly. In jail, we were waiting for the reports of police firing and killing, but all went off peacefully.

On the other hand my birthday in July, my fifth in prison, was celebrated turbulently. There were riots in the Reformatory Jail; the jail records were burned by angry détenus demanding improved conditions. The Bihar Military Police were called in to deal with them. In Phulwarisharif Prison Camp, near Patna, eighteen people were injured in clashes between warders and prisoners, and in Bhagalpur Jail student détenus were beaten up by warders. The shock waves were felt in our own jail. There was yet another frenzy of searching. I do not think they really expected to find anything; it was just a punishment for the people's opposition to the government.

In the midst of this turmoil there seemed an ever-diminishing chance that our trial would ever start. A warder posted from Jamshedpur said there were now over a thousand prisoners in that jail. Thirty old men were locked in the cell that had been mine. Two hundred prisoners were kept in what had been our courtroom.

Between the professor's sojourns, the next-door cell was occupied by another MISA détenue, a former Member of Parliament for the Socialist Party. She came from a landowning family that had mechanized its farms and enjoyed, she informed me, a net annual income of fifty thousand rupees. One day, she waved her arms towards the expanse of garden around us and said: 'Do you call this prison? This is not a prison. For the first eight years of my married life I was confined to two rooms and a courtyard at the back of the house.' Like many Hindu women of the traditionalist wealthy classes, she had spent much of her married life in purdah. Luckily her husband, after the death of his father, had allowed her to go out of the house, and eventually to join him in politics.

This woman was a devout Hindu and spent hours each day walking round the yard reading some holy scripture from a book in her hand. I admired her serenity; but, like most of the other political prisoners, she was sympathetic but remote, and did not associate with the other women. In dress, she was austere, though her saree was of the finest quality handloom; she ate little, but what she did eat had to be of the best. She had visited England some years previously with a parliamentary delegation and told me she had brought a television set back with her. It was still standing idle in her country house, because there was no service outside Delhi and parts of Punjab. I thought it an amusing status symbol.

During the months from March to August, I hardly wrote a word in my diary or a detailed letter to my family. My mind was too troubled to enable me to concentrate. One of the occasions that did inspire me to put pen to paper was when Indian scientists exploded a nuclear device in May that year. The irony of it filled me to bursting point; people were starving, no effective irrigation system existed in more than twenty per cent of the country, disease was rampant and seemingly uncontrollable, India had the biggest debts of any country in the world, there was no electricity in most of the villages, no proper drinking water in many of the towns, over seventy per cent of the population was illiterate, and the government was spending millions of rupees on exploding nuclear devices and boasting of 'achievement'. The real achievement would be measured only when the explosion could be seen to have benefited the people.

One day in July a wardress told me that a recently arrived Naxalite prisoner had been dipped bodily into boiling water by police who had arrested him. A prisoner heard the Superintendent reprimanding the jail doctor for giving expensive medicines to sick Naxalites and thus strengthening them to fight the government. There were press reports of torture on female Naxalites in Presidency Jail, Calcutta, where Kalpana was being detained. In three Calcutta jails, forty-two Naxalites went on hunger strike for nearly a month for improvements in their conditions. I could feel the same building-up of tension as in 1971, and was not surprised to read that Naxalites were once more being killed in 'encounters' with police.

At the beginning of August we found a wild kitten in the undergrowth of our vegetable plot. I tied it to the bars of my cell, hoping to tame it. If it could be persuaded to stay with us it might kill the rats that destroyed a large proportion of our potato, tomato, bean and maize crops each year. I kept it tied up for ten days and its mother came every night to feed it. After each meeting, the kitten cried plaintively. In her cell across the courtyard Moti was alarmed on hearing the cries. She became convinced that the kitten was a witch; this idea was reinforced when the mother cat slipped into her cell one night when she was asleep and stole some *chapatis* she had left lying in her dish. In addition, the attention we lavished on the kitten and the food we gave it aroused her jealousy. She got angrier each day and often stood outside our cell raging at me and the kitten for hours on end.

One morning I had gone to scour our dishes and was just returning to the cell when I heard a horrible screaming. I dropped the aluminium dishes and dashed up the steps. Moti was sitting there with the cat in her lap, her hands around its throat, about to strangle it. When she saw me, she let go immediately and, assuming a disarmingly innocent grin, said: 'I was just stroking her. Isn't she lovely?' I was at a loss for what to do. I could not just kill the kitten, which by that time was quite tame; on the other hand, if I kept it, Moti might try to kill it again. I decided to let things go for a time and hope that Moti would quieten down.

But the heat and humidity of the monsoon season and the aggravation she felt with the cat made her more hot-headed than ever. She often packed up all the bits and pieces she had collected, scraps of cloth, hairpins, rings, ribbons, old pieces of string, dried chick peas, rusty bits of metal and bent nails, tied them into a Dick Whittington bundle and marched to the gate, rattling the iron bolt and demanding to be let out: she was going home. 'How long do you expect me to stay here? I'm going back to my own country. Come and open the gate. I'm going!' she would bawl. One night she prepared all her things as usual for her departure. As the Chief Head Warder left the ward after counting us next morning, she tried to follow him. Afraid that he might hit her for trying to 'escape', I tried to restrain her. Furious with me, she turned back and twisted my wrist. Unfortunately, the warder had seen her. He turned and raised his stick to hit her. She was immediately cowed and docile, and started pleading, 'No, sir, don't hit me.' But he had already started. He struck her time and time again, pushing, shoving and bellowing at her to get back to her cell. It was pathetic. Moti was whimpering and bending to touch his feet and begging him to stop hitting her, but he seemed to have gone mad. At last we managed to intervene and stop him; but not until he had struck at least twenty blows on Moti's arms, legs and back. She crept into her cell, where she lay whimpering and moaning like a kicked dog. Her body was covered in weals and she could hardly walk for two days. Every time she heard the warder's voice, she buried herself under her blankets in the corner of the cell. She refused to emerge even to go to the lavatory unless someone accompanied her. She kept saying to me,

'Don't let him hit me again, *Beti*.' I promised her I would not.

I blamed myself for the whole incident, for keeping a cat that made her angry, for letting the warder see her grab my wrist, for not being able to prevent him from striking her. I was no longer able to look him in the face without hating him. Yet it was futile to think that he was conscious of having done any-thing wrong. The law of the big stick was the only one he knew; he did not have an inkling that there might be any other way of controlling prisoners. Nobody among the warders and wardresses had more than a vague idea of jail rules, they received no training apart from some superficial military drill, and were plunged into their jobs to manage as best they could and keep the prisoners quiet without bothering their superiors. No ques-tions were asked about the methods they employed.

At about that time, the Chief Head Warder's favourite, a villain who worked in the jail office, went on a fortnight's parole, taking with him 9,000 rupees he was said to have saved within the space of eleven months. The wardresses were earning just over 200 rupees a month and the Jailer's salary was less than 1,000. Shortly after this news was relayed to me, I met with an example of what happened to those mates who did not fit in with the general pattern of things in jail. Among the convicts who came every evening with the hospital food and medicine for the sick was one called Ramesh, who was particularly liked by the women because, unlike the others, he was scrupulous in administering whatever the doctor had prescribed for them. Whenever they asked him what caste he belonged to, he would say: 'I am a human being. What more do you need to know?' One evening he beckoned to me and said, 'I won't be coming any more, *Didi*. I'm going to work in the jail garden.' There were tears in his eyes. I knew he was due for release in a few weeks and was planning to set up a dispensary, using the know-ledge he had gained in jail, so I could not understand why he should be wanting to go and work in the garden. But, the duty warder was watching us and I could not question him further.

However, it never took us long to find out all the jail scandals.

We heard next day from some other convicts that some of Ramesh's rivals in the hospital had bribed the Chief Head Warder to send him to work elsewhere, because he was too honest and was depriving them of their 'income'. When the doctor next came to our ward, we asked him to intervene with the Jailer on Ramesh's behalf, but he simply shrugged his shoulders and said, 'What do you want me to do? I need him in the hospital, he is a good worker. But this has been done by the Chief Head Warder and the Jailer themselves. If I say anything they'll find an excuse to transfer me too.' We kept up a half-hearted protest for a few days by refusing medicines and supplies from the hospital, but nobody really cared whether we took them or not and we soon gave up. I was afraid to say too much on Ramesh's behalf, although I really wanted to help him, because I knew that if I appeared unduly concerned about him the authorities would become suspicious and probably accuse him of being a Naxalite. If that happened, he might end his prison term in fetters.

We did not see Ramesh again until the day he was released. That morning, he took the risk of coming to say good-bye to us. We did not even know his full name, much less why he was in jail, but we thought of him as a dear friend. In jail, a smile, a kind gesture or a few pleasant words assume a meaning far deeper than in the world outside where one is free to indulge in un-inhibited human relationships.

After Rajkumari was released and Somri transferred, my cell was shared by two young women, Dulali and Kormi. Dulali was a Harijan and had worked as a lavatory cleaner at a copper mine not far from Jamshedpur. She had been arrested on an attempted murder charge after intervening to stop some men who were fighting in the street outside her house. She could not have been more than thirty-five, and looked younger, but was the mother of seven children; her eldest son was already married. She was small, wiry and extremely tough and energetic, and reminded me of a Cockney charlady. She told me her father had been unfortunate enough to have ten daughters, and, not being able to afford 'good' marriages for them, had had to marry them off to any man who would take them. Dulali had been married to a man older than herself who already had a wife unable to bear children. Fortunately, he was good to both women. Dulali considered herself the equal of any man and would stand no nonsense anyway. As she and her husband were both working and lived in quarters attached to the mine, they ate fairly well. But she told me that her sister, after working for twenty-five years at the same place and qualifying for a bonus, had suddenly been declared 'unfit' and made redundant without one rupee's compensation.

Having been used, from childhood, to being considered 'untouchable', Dulali was not convinced that I was really willing to eat food that she had cooked. For weeks she showed extreme reluctance even to go near the fire. When I did persuade her to prepare our meal, saying that I wanted to do some study or sewing, she used to keep interrupting me to ask what to do next. One day I said, 'Look, don't pretend you can't cook. How did you manage to bring up seven children? I'll eat whatever you give me.' After that she cooked perfect curries.

Another day we were given some watery yoghurt, a once-a-year treat reserved for a special festival. I was doing something and asked Dulali to go and collect my share together with her own. She came back feeling hurt because the duty warder had said, 'What, do you mean to tell me that Tyler eats food touched by a lavatory cleaner?' It was a pity he had gone away, otherwise I would have told him straight away what I thought of his comment: like the rest of the staff, though he might find Harijans' food too dirty to eat, he was quite happy to accept the bribes they gave him.

Accustomed all her life to eating other people's left-overs, Dulali never wasted a thing; she would clear up pips, skins, anything left on our plates – not that there was ever much. She considered anything suitable for her consumption: burnt food, stale food, rotten food, anything that would not actually poison her. Whenever there was any dirty work to do, the wardresses called on Dulali to do it. There was nothing that aroused her revulsion: on the contrary, she found it natural that she should wash bloodstained and soiled clothes, clean lavatories, and clear up vomit. She told me that some of the people she had worked for 'purified' their houses after she had been there. Ironically, she was one of the cleanest people I ever met. She had a knack of polishing our stone floor until it gleamed, with no cleaning materials except an old piece of rag and cold water. The one thing that was calculated to make her bad-tempered was if she was forced, for some reason, to miss her daily bath.

Kormi was a different type altogether. A Hindu peasant of the Burhi caste, about midway on the social scale as far as I could gather, she was very conscious of her status. As we sat eating together she would sometimes say, 'I could never be doing this outside. We only eat food cooked by Brahmans and Rajputs.' Dulali lived in an industrial area, had been to the cinema several times a week and knew about aeroplanes, sky-scrapers and various types of machinery, but Kormi had never once been to the 'silema', as she called it, nor even seen a railway line or a bus. Poverty alone had driven her out of the house to go and work on a local farmer's fields or on government relief schemes. Naturally, coming from this background, she was narrow-minded, but she was also goodhearted and reliable and, though slow, very thorough in her work.

Kormi's life had been tragic. She had given birth to five children, only one of whom had survived infancy, and had been widowed while still not much over twenty. In accordance with the custom prevalent in that part of Bihar, she had been taken by her husband's younger brother as a second wife. Though unwilling, she had had little choice in the matter; a local land-owner to whom her husband had owed money wanted to sell her into a brothel to make good his loan; the only alternative was to agree to live with her brother-in-law. Soon she was preg-nant again, but, goaded by her jealous sister-in-law and de-pressed at the thought of another stillborn child, had contrived to do away with the unborn foetus. Her sister-in-law, glad of the chance to get rid of her rival, had got the matter reported to the local police, and Kormi had been arrested on a murder charge. She sometimes suffered severe abdominal pains, probably a result of the inexpert abortion and lack of subsequent medical care, and was mentally quite unco-ordinated, which was understandable considering the experiences she had been through. At night she often woke up and called to me to feel her pulse, telling me that her heart was jumping about. Nearly every night she talked in her sleep. I was able to sympathize with Kormi when she stated quite emphatically that she never wanted to leave jail, because, at least, while she was there, she was sure of not becoming pregnant any more.

Apart from her other qualities, she was a rich source of village lore. She was convinced that her children had been killed by a witch and that her mother-in-law's ghost had made her husband die of smallpox. She also informed us in all seriousness one day that women in her 'country' had given birth to pumpkins, marrows, elephants and snakes. Though Dulali and I collapsed with laughter at the time, afterwards, when I started thinking about what she really meant, I realized that she was probably referring to misshapen foetuses and deformed babies.

Something that happened one day made me realize how little I still understood about caste. One morning, Kormi was quarrelling with another woman at the water tap, and Dulali went to restrain her, whereupon she diverted her wrath to Dulali herself. Dulali was never one to put up with unjustified attacks, and ended up by slapping Kormi round the face. The effect was dramatic. Kormi burst into tears, though the blow had not hurt her. She sobbed inconsolably for most of the day. Dulali asked me to go and apologize on her behalf and make Kormi stop crying. I tried, but with no success. It was not until Dulali explained to me that I understood the real cause of her tears. It was not the fact that the slap had hurt her, but that she, a caste Hindu, had been struck by a Harijan. It was a terrible blow to her pride. I was astounded. I had thought that, apart from Kormi's occasional remark, the three of us had managed to overcome the bounds of caste. We cooked and ate together, wore each other's clothes, shared the same blankets and utensils. I had not realized how close the question of caste pride still was to the surface of Kormi's mind. She did eventually get over her upset, but it took considerable explanation and coaxing, not to mention an abject apology from Dulali, who had not been at fault at all, for her 'sin'.

Many of the women prisoners had never seen white bread before. The prison bread, prescribed for those too ill to digest chick peas, was grey, sour and often half raw, but, nevertheless, considered a luxury. Once, when Kormi was ill, the doctor allowed her five days' supply of dry bread for breakfast. I noticed that, instead of eating it, she was wrapping it up in a piece of cloth and storing it away. When I asked her why, she told me she was saving it to take to court because her son was coming to see her on her next date. I pointed out that that was still three weeks away, and that the bread would be as hard as rock by then. She said it did not matter; he could soak it in water, at least it would be something better than his usual food. He would think it a treat. When she did go to court next time, she took not only the bread but all her meagre savings to give to the boy to buy new clothes.

One of the prisoners who had been in Hazaribagh even longer than I was Birsi, a wrinkled and ancient-looking woman of the same caste as Rajkumari. She was very timid and was unable to assert herself in the daily bickerings over who was to cook first, get the biggest piece of soap or a second helping of food, so she invariably landed at the back of the queue. In March that year her husband had died in jail, after the two of them had been there over four years waiting for a land dispute to be settled. They had been charged with harvesting paddy on a piece of land they claimed was theirs, but which a rich peasant in their village said was his. After her 'old man's' death, Birsi was more nervous and pitiable than ever. I noticed that she saved all her rice ration now that flour was being issued once more, and lived on two *chapatis* a day. She was always among the first to sell her soap and oil. She never spent any of her savings on nice things to eat, new clothes, bangles or nail varnish, as some of the other women did. I thought perhaps that she was pining for her husband and the daughter she had left at home, and urged her to eat properly. With prices rising all the time it was futile to save; even if she was released her few rupees would buy next to nothing. At least she could buy a saree and save it for her daughter. I suppose my nagging was getting on her nerves, because she finally decided that she would have to explain the reason for her frugality.

On leaving jail, she said, she would have a lot of expenses. She would have to pay for the religious rites that had not been performed after her husband's death. On top of that, she would have to sacrifice a goat, feed the local Brahmans and give them presents, give money to the village headman and council and probably stand the whole village a feast in order to buy back the caste she had lost on coming to jail. If she failed to do this, she would be an outcaste, neither allowed to enter anyone's house nor to welcome them to hers. Water would be brought from the well by others and left outside her threshold. In order to avoid this humiliation, she was half starving herself to save enough money to perform the necessary rites and penances.

Birsi's story was corroborated by other prisoners. It turned out that nearly all the women were putting aside some money to help buy back their social standing when they returned to their villages. This was a new angle on the old problem of a prisoner's rehabilitation into society!

At the beginning of August, I was taken to the office to meet three of my co-defendants who were being transferred to Jamshedpur for the first of the seven trials that were now to be held. In addition to the joint case against all of us, separate charges had been lodged against various groups and individuals among us. They promised to make arrangements for our defence. The Superintendent assured me that I would soon be following them. On the last Sunday in August 1974, I was transferred once more from Hazaribagh to Jamshedpur, 'for trial'.

## 12. Dhatingna

From my point of view, the journey that time was enjoyable. The young officer in charge of the police escort let me sit next to him in the front of the jeep. The driver drove fast and the cool air of the monsoon evening filled my lungs and cleared my brain. For my co-defendants, on the contrary, that and each subsequent journey from one jail to another was agony. They were transported in fetters, handcuffed in pairs and tied together in fours with ropes around the waist. In this condition they had somehow to crowd into a space meant for half their number, and then all their possessions were thrown on top of them. It was worst of all for those who suffered from travel sickness.

Bina was expecting me but it was night when I arrived, and I was only able to greet her through the bars of the cell where she was locked with over forty other women and a dozen children. Next morning she brought me the gifts she had been keeping for me, two sweets she had been given a fortnight before on Independence Day. She was now 'matine', and looked much thinner and more serious than before. She took me by the hand to go and see the other prisoners. I immediately noticed that there was a far more relaxed atmosphere than there had been under the Procuress. Ten months had passed, but old Gulabi was still there. Heera's little boy was now over a year old, but weak and puny. Shortly before he had almost died from measles.

The trial was due to start on 28 August. That morning, I prepared to go to court. As the Judge had rejected the Prosecution's request for the proceedings to take place inside the jail, I was expecting to be taken to the local courts. Shortly after ten o'clock, I was called to the office to meet a Secretary from the Deputy High Commission. He was faintly surprised to discover that I had not been informed that the court appearance had been postponed until 3 October. The five cases still pending against me and various of my co-defendants were to be amalgamated at the request of our lawyer, who was trying to speed up the whole proceedings, pointing out that all the cases involved the same witnesses, the same dates and similar charges. The hearing had been postponed to allow time for preparation of the amalgamated trial.

I was used to delays and false rumours, but that time I had really believed the trial was going to start, and I was angry and disappointed at the further postponement. All at once the five weeks till 3 October seemed an interminably long time to wait. Further annoyance was to come. Due to the continuing disturbances all over Bihar, there were no Military Police available to set up the camps that usually surrounded prisons where Naxalites were held, and it was decided that, for security reasons, we would be sent back to Hazaribagh. The thought of packing up all my books again into two khaki bags, to be thrown into the police van and jolted about all the way to Hazaribagh, seemed more than I could cope with. I made up my mind not to go. On the morning we were due to be transferred, I lied to the wardress, telling her I had diarrhoea and stomach pains and was unable to get up. The doctor had no choice but to certify me sick, and I was left in Jamshedpur while my co-defendants went back to Hazaribagh. I was glad to have the chance of spending more time with Bina who, in my absence, had persevered and made so much progress in her studies that she was able to read quite fluently.

A few days later, I learned from a sympathetic warder that the Special Public Prosecutor, sent from Patna to conduct our case because he was renowned for 'getting convictions', was using his month's grace period to attempt to persuade government officials in Patna to instruct that our trials be held inside jail. Electric fans were being re-fitted in our former courtroom in anticipation that his request would be granted. He was also trying to reverse the Judge's order for amalgamation of the cases. He wanted as many separate trials as possible; the longer the whole thing lasted, the more profitable it would be to him. The warder told me to be prepared for further conspiracies. The Special Public Prosecutor was extremely annoyed with the Judge, who had refused the offer of free transport on condition that he hold court inside jail. Someone else told me that the SPP had promised various local dignitaries a feast if he managed to get us convicted.

Other forces were also at work. The attempts by my friends to draw attention to the case had aroused the interest of the press, and correspondents were present in Jamshedpur for the projected court hearings. In addition, in the month of September that year, Amnesty International published a report on the conditions of political prisoners in the jails of West Bengal, mentioning that there were fifteen to twenty thousand of them in that state alone. Though the Indian Government refuted all the charges, there is no doubt that the Amnesty report drew international attention to the plight of political prisoners in India for the first time.

The 3 October was a repetition of 28 August. I again prepared to go to court, only to be informed by the same British official that the Superintendent of Police had declared himself unable to provide a police escort to accompany us to court. All available police had been deployed to deal with the three-day general strike that had been called in Bihar. The SPP asked for a long adjournment of the hearing, pending restoration of 'normalcy'. The Judge, observing that, whatever the conditions in Bihar as a whole might be, the situation in Jamshedpur was perfectly normal, gave instructions for us to be produced in court without fail on Monday, 7 October.

On the following Monday we were taken to court in a police van built to carry twenty-two people. There were thirty-six of us and about a dozen armed police in it. We sat from ten a.m. until two thirty waiting to be taken into court. It was unbearably hot and airless. At about noon our lawyer came to inform us that the SPP had lodged yet another petition. This time he was asking the District Judge to transfer the whole trial to another court, declaring himself to have no confidence in the present judge, whom he accused of 'placating Naxalites'. He had given grounds for this accusation: the Judge had allowed one teenage boy's mother to talk to him and give him food in court; he had refused to hold the trial inside jail; he had granted legal aid to two prisoners who had not appointed a lawyer; and he had met an official of the British High Commission privately in his chambers. The case was to be adjourned until the petition had been heard in the District Court at Chaibasa. That afternoon's court appearance was a five-minute formality.

The insinuation that a British diplomat had met the judge privately for some unethical purpose naturally upset the Foreign Office. The Secretary from Calcutta had only gone to find out how long the trial was likely to last, and the Prosecutor's assistant had been present throughout the meeting. I am convinced that this final step on the part of the Prosecution caused the Foreign Office to intensify its efforts on my behalf.

The judge of our case prepared a statement for the District Judge, refuting the allegations that he was placating Naxalites and pointing out that whereas he was interested only in holding a prompt and fair trial according to law, he was being hindered at every turn by the manoeuvrings of the Prosecution. He went further, concluding that any judge trying the case would have to contend with the same delaying tactics, as the SPP's main interest was to prolong the trial as much as possible in order to earn the maximum fees. This was an extraordinary accusation to be made by a judge against the official representative of the State.

The hearing was again adjourned until 27 November, after the Durga Puja holidays, and it seemed likely that I would have to return to Hazaribagh until then. The High Commission officials present on that day assured me that they would be approaching the Central Government for a speedy trial without further delays. But one of the jail officers told me not to hold out any hopes; the Prosecution's transfer petition was bound to be granted: the SPP and his assistants were all Bhumihar Brahmans, and the District Judge belonged to the same caste. He would be sure to listen to their side of the story.

That same night, just after dark, the Head Warder told me

that I was to prepare to go to Hazaribagh right away. I was furious. They were always so quick, it seemed, to do what suited them, yet when it came to putting us on trial there were any number of reasons for delaying. My health had been deteriorating for some time and I had difficulty in seeing properly. I certainly did not feel like groping around in the dim light of an oil lamp to find my books and clothing. I was not going to Hazaribagh that night. They would have to wait. One after another, the warders and office staff came to persuade me to go. I ignored them, lay down and pretended to be asleep. In the end they gave up and sent my fellow accused back to their cells for the night. We went to Hazaribagh next morning.

Because of our hasty departure, we had been unable to consult with our lawyer. At the end of October he came to Hazaribagh, and for the first time I was allowed a prolonged and unhindered discussion with him and some of my fellow defendants, out of hearing of the Special Branch. This unique opportunity was due not so much to their goodwill but to the fact that the jail office was crowded with MISA détenus, including Karpoori Thakur, who had been the Bihar Chief Minister earlier in my imprisonment. Now he had joined his former prisoners. No wonder the warders were usually anxious to placate political prisoners of all shades. One never knew whom the vicissitudes of life might bring into power.

The lawyer had been investigating the sums of government money spent on our case. It amounted to thirty thousand rupees, apart from what it was costing to keep us in jail. He had also discovered that nepotism had played the major role in the appointments of the three Prosecution lawyers. All had influential relatives in government service. The transfer petition was still pending, but, he assured us, with the information he now had to hand and the efforts being made on our behalf, things were beginning to go our way.

Soon after the Movement had started in March, its leadership had been assumed by Jayprakash Narayan, a veteran Gandhian and a staunch anti-communist, though he had once belonged to the Socialist Party. As the movement continued, leadership seemed to be falling increasingly into the hands of right-wing parties who were concentrating their attention on demanding dissolution of the Legislative Assembly and new parliamentary elections which, I was sure, would do nothing but bring into power another corrupt government. Though it still commanded tremendous support among certain sections of the population, I felt that the Movement had deteriorated. There was no apparent long-term strategy that could have brought about a real change in conditions. Both sides were bogged down in day-to-day struggles and counter-struggles without any clear plan. The concepts of 'total revolution' and 'classless democracy' put forward by Narayan himself seemed abstract and unfeasible.

Crowds of Narayan's female followers filled the female ward. In the afternoons they sang songs and performed dances in praise of the non-mechanized village life which they believed to be the solution to India's problems. They had none of the affectations of other middle-class prisoners I had seen, were simple in habits and willing to work; some had deliberately broken with tradition by marrying outside their caste. Despite all this, my impression was that they were a kind of sect which, though in some ways receptive to new ideas, was unable to reach out to embrace the vast sections of the population who were suffering most.

There were one or two exceptions among the Movement prisoners. One of these we called *Dadi*, Granny. She was a toothless old Brahman peasant. Her poverty proved that I had been wrong in equating caste too rigidly with class. Although in general the tribal people and Harijans are the victims of most injustice, and overall the poorest sections of the whole population, there are poor people in all castes. Dadi was friendly and generous. She and her only son had joined the Movement out of deference to the local landlord, who, for his own reasons, had urged them to participate. They owed him money and had little choice in the matter. They had been arrested for squatting on the railway line during the general strike.

She was a widow and the family had no land. Her son earned 105 rupees a month labouring on the railway tracks. At that time, the price of rice was almost four rupees a kilogram, and his earnings were quite insufficient to feed himself, wife, sister and mother. In addition he had to pay off the debt he owed the landlord, incurred at the time of his other sister's wedding. It was not considered right for Brahman women to work in the fields, though sometimes they did housework and cooking for wealthy families in their village. Often, Dadi went hungry.

She said: 'I spend the days in merriment and so forget my hunger. If I feel very hungry I mix some salt with water and drink it to stave off the pangs. At night we have one meal of *chapatis* with a little lentil soup or vegetable. We make four *chapatis*. My son gets two and the girls one each. I have no separate share but eat a little from each of their portions.' Her son was labouring seven days a week, fifty-two weeks a year, to maintain this existence. Dadi stayed longer than the other Movement people. In the end the landlord did arrange her bail. The loan they had taken from him was increased, and the family had incurred another burden of debt.

In November, I was pleasantly surprised when the consul who had gone on leave returned from Britain having, as he promised, visited my parents. They had sent some gifts which he kindly passed on to me. There were sweets, chocolate, biscuits, hand cream, and, most welcome of all, underwear, which my mother had somehow divined was something I was badly in need of. The sweets and biscuits were soon finished; after sharing them round, I sat and gobbled my own portion like Bessie Bunter. Some of the other women were like me and devoured any little extras that came their way without any sense of proportion. Others did the opposite, hoarding their share of the goodies until they were almost unfit for consumption. Neither method had a very salutary effect on the digestion. There was generally a wave of sickness and diarrhoea after every holiday and festival when we were given food somewhat better than our usual diet.

At the end of that month I was again taken to Jamshedpur, but as the transfer petition had still not been heard, the case was adjourned yet again, this time until 1 February. In view of the

long adjournment, I expected to be sent straight back to Hazaribagh, and, sure enough, next morning the warder told me to
prepare to go. I sat there the whole day, books and clothing
ready packed, but nothing happened. The next day was the
same. On the third day, I discovered what the matter was. All
police vans in the town were out of order. This was nothing new.
One day the police van had broken down outside the court and
we had been taken back to jail in an army lorry. When I asked
a driver why police vehicles were always breaking down, he said
that no mechanic in Jamshedpur would repair them because
they knew they would not be paid. Nearly every time we went
from Jamshedpur to Hazaribagh there were long delays along
the road due to some fault or other in one of the vehicles.

Eventually we returned to Hazaribagh, that time just before
Christmas. Two days later, I was visited once more by the British
Consul. After being assured by the Inspector General of Police
in Patna that I was still in Jamshedpur and would be there for
Christmas, he had gone to that town to find that I had been
transferred to Hazaribagh a couple of days previously. Having a
car and time at his disposal, he was able to continue the journey
to Hazaribagh. Members of Amalendu's family and people who
came to visit my co-defendants were not always so lucky. Several
times that year family members came to see me, only to discover
that I was not in the jail where they had assumed me to be.
Owing to the great distances involved, they had to return to
Calcutta without seeing me. For friends and family in England,
it was worse. The shifts from jail to jail totally disrupted even
the limited correspondence we had previously kept up, and they
rarely knew where I was at any particular moment.

On 3 January 1975, one of the office writers came to tell
us that L. N. Mishra, the Union Minister for Railways, had
been assassinated in Samastipur, North Bihar. Even among those
prisoners who had heard of him, there was no hint of regret. It
was Mishra who had been responsible for the savage repression
during the railwaymen's strike and upon whose instructions
thousands of workers had lost both jobs and homes. The assas-
sination had repercussions on our uncertain existence. There had

been, the papers reported, seven hundred plain-clothes police on duty at the railway station where the Minister was killed; now there were bitter accusations of police inefficiency, in particular on the part of the Intelligence Branch. As if to prove themselves, the Special Branch men posted in the jail suddenly 'discovered' another escape plot, and there were once again searches for arms and explosives. Nothing was found. But at least what I called the 'Save Our Jobs' campaign had succeeded; they had come up with the 'intelligence' that they were employed to supply.

Early in 1975, we were asked to look after a beggar child whom some convicts had found at the gate of Chandwara Camp Jail, crawling in the dust with his begging bowl, unable to stand up. They had persuaded the Superintendent to admit him into the jail, and undoubtedly this had prevented his dying from starvation. When I first saw him, he was able to toddle, though the enormous size of his belly often made him overbalance. It had swollen to these proportions as soon as he started eating regular meals. Apart from this huge belly and his extraordinarily large head, the rest of his body was puny and stunted, his bones light and frail. His decaying teeth were covered with a yellow crust. Two loose milk teeth indicated that he was six or seven years old, but he was unable to talk; his attempts at conversation came out as grunts, possibly because no one had talked to him enough for him to learn to speak. On the other hand he understood everything we said to him. Never having been used to regular food, he stretched out his hand automatically whenever he saw anything edible, even though his stomach was already full. To him, food was something to be eaten whenever and wherever and in whatever quantities one could find it. He was very keen to take the medicines the doctor gave him for his malnutrition, liver trouble and worms, seeing them too as another form of food.

As a result of his battle for survival, he was tough, stubborn and often disobedient, but frequently came and climbed into our laps and clung to us, demanding the affection which he had obviously never encountered before. Tears would roll down my cheeks as I hugged him. Little by little we taught him to wash himself, clean his teeth (this caused him a lot of pain and he protested) and to tell us he wanted to go to the lavatory so that we could wash his bottom. In spite of my remonstrations, the other women called him *Dhatingna* – greedy guts. This was not meant unkindly. On the contrary, it was proof of their straightforwardness that they were able to call people by their characteristics without any sense of criticism or mockery. They always called Prokash's mother 'Cripple' and Moti 'Mad One' because that is what they were. I named Dhatingna my 'Minister', because, paradoxically, his fat belly reminded me of the bloated paunches of high government officials. His future was uncertain, but several prisoners had expressed the desire to take him home with them when they were released. Inevitably he would become a servant in one of their households, an unpaid chattel, but at least he would not starve.

On the journey to Jamshedpur for the next court appearance, I saw an accident. A car speeding past our convoy knocked down a cyclist a little way ahead of us, and drove on without stopping. The young officer in charge of our escort, after some initial hesitation, obeyed the call of duty and ordered our driver to overtake and stop the hit-and-run car. Our jeep pulled up in front of the stopped car, and timidly but officiously the officer approached it. Four tall, menacing and prosperous-looking characters in dark glasses emerged from it, strolled threateningly towards him and, before he had a chance to open his mouth, informed him that the cyclist had 'fallen off'. Immediately the police officer beat a fearful retreat, muttering, 'Yes, yes, he fell off, I saw it, yes, yes, probably drunk, these villagers drink like fish . . .' The chorus was taken up by the other policemen, who understood full well the demands of the moment. 'Yes, yes, he fell off, I saw him . . .' 'Drunkard . . .' The bleeding cyclist was left on the road to his fate, to recover or die, to get up or be run over by the next vehicle. He was poor and did not matter. Those in the car were wealthy, perhaps powerful, and could not possibly be prosecuted for hit and run. After all, one's job was more important than a poor, injured and abandoned human being . . .

*

That time, though the Special Public Prosecutor's attempt to change the judge had, surprisingly, failed, there was still no progress in the case, as the petition against the amalgamation of the trials had not yet been heard in Patna High Court. We obtained permission to stay in Jamshedpur ten days for consultations with our lawyer and members of the Bihar Legal Aid Committee, who had agreed to help us out with costs. If they had not done so, we would have had great difficulty in meeting the costs of the complicated and prolonged legal proceedings. I was only afraid that our lawyer, Uday Mishra, would lose the rest of his practice if our case dragged on too long and demanded too much of his time.

When the ten days were up, there was the usual problem of finding suitable transport back to Hazaribagh. Eventually, a state bus was requisitioned. As I left the office to climb into the waiting vehicle, I noticed an old Bengali lady, the mother of one of my fellow accused, weeping. After waiting since morning to see her son, on top of the long journey from Calcutta, she had been allowed only a few words in passing when he was summoned to join the bus. She was crying at the sight of the iron fetters on his legs. Through the bus window he called out to her: 'You don't mind having bangles on your wrists, why should I mind having bracelets round my ankles?' I was deeply impressed by this effort to cheer up his old mother. Even the High Commission officials had commented on the alert and cheerful attitude of the men in my case when they saw them in court, and I often had occasion to feel profound respect for the way in which they bore their difficulties.

The journey that day was memorable. From my vantage point in the front seat, I had a commanding view over the countryside of Chhotanagpur. The sudden sight of a road between hills and the broad horizon all at once opened up poignant memories of past freedom; but soon I was concentrating on absorbing all I could of the outside world in the limited time available. We drove past fields that had been left to sun and sky after the harvest had been gathered from them, waiting for the Spring rains that would prepare them for the next sowing. Already in

February it was hot and dusty. We crossed rivers that were, before summer had even started, no more than trickles in a parched sea of sand. The sky was colourless, the sun like a magnetic eye. Children were fishing in minute pools, tearing off reeds to use in their play in field and forest. I thought of the sorrow and suffering, the tenacity that was hidden behind the walls of the mud and thatch huts, in the tiny dark space that was home for families whose life meant no more than survival. Occasionally we passed the fenced-in compound of a brick house, to keep in purdah the brides and daughters of the prosperous. Military camps, with their trucks and rifles and electrified fencing, reminded me that India was also in the twentieth century. Sometimes we passed through a town, swarming, insanitary, at once mediaeval and modern, the road lined with workshops, factories and garages. At last we came to the hills of Hazaribagh, a vast expanse of valley and coalmine and jungle. I felt a longing to reach out and touch the trees, forgetting momentarily the forest of rifles that separated me from them.

We arrived before locking time, and I was greeted by women and children as if I had been away eleven years instead of eleven days. One piece of sad news marred the welcome: my kitten had been drowned in a well in the male sector. It was the first time I had left her behind in Hazaribagh when I went to Jamshedpur.

One morning the sweeper who had recently been delegated to clean our latrines, an under-trial prisoner whose bold attitude I had already noticed, told me that he and the other sweepers earned four annas (one quarter of a rupee) a day, which accumulated in the office and was supposed to be paid to them when they left the jail. The previous day one of his friends had been transferred to another jail and the Jailer had refused to give him his earnings, saying that his papers were not in order. When the man protested that he had worked nine months for nothing, the Jailer replied, 'Well, what are you going to do about it?' and pocketed, presumably, the hard-earned rupees that the prisoner had hoped would help him fight his case.

This sweeper of ours suffered the same fate as other prisoners who dared to speak out against the system. One day he went to court and, together with some other prisoners, including several Naxalites, shouted slogans in the lock-up against the corruption prevailing both in jail and in the legal system. The next morning, another prisoner came to clean the latrines. When we asked what had happened to the other man, the new sweeper just said, 'He's misbehaved.' After repeated questioning, he said the other man had stolen some money from another prisoner and had been put in solitary confinement. I was almost sure it was a cooked-up story to punish him for shouting slogans in court about the jail staff.

At that time, the Superintendent was often absent. He was due for retirement, and, reluctant to relinquish his profitable post, was trying to persuade his superiors to let him stay on another year. There had been protests from those waiting for promotion to his job, and for several months the post remained vacant while it was being decided whether or not he should stay. At one stage, there was no Superintendent in any of the four Central Jails in that region of Bihar. The struggles for promotion to these posts took a simple form: all the interested candidates made trips to Patna, pockets bulging, in order to vie with each other in greasing palms in the right places. This fact was openly admitted to me by people on the jail staff. They told me as a joke, not with any intention to malign anybody. To them, it was the accepted way of doing things. They might not like it, but they had to live with it.

Under the relaxed rule of Guruwari, the old tribal matine who had replaced Balko, I had more chance to speak to the male prisoners who came to our ward. Hari had been bringing my rations to me ever since I first came to Hazaribagh, but I knew very little about him except that he had nearly finished a twenty-year sentence. One day I asked him about his family. At first he was suspicious, then all at once started talking about himself as if he wanted to tell someone what was on his mind. He was a middle peasant; his family had sufficient land to feed themselves through the year, but with little surplus. One year their crops had been deliberately ruined by some men hired by a big land-owner in the area who wanted to force them into mortgaging their fertile land to him. One evening soon afterwards, Hari came home from the fields to find that there was no food in the house and his old mother, who had been starving herself to feed the family, had collapsed from hunger. There and then he decided that he was going to kill the man responsible for their plight. As the eldest son, he felt it was his duty to avenge his family. After killing the landlord, he had surrendered to the police.

Hari said he had never regretted his deed for a minute. With the enemy out of the way, his brothers were able to cultivate their land in peace. But, now the time for his release was near, he was apprehensive, wondering what would happen when he went back to his village. I realized he was thinking that he might be killed in revenge for the murder he had committed. In the countryside, memories were long, and years spent behind government bars were no guarantee that village justice had been satisfied.

My next trip to Jamshedpur lasted only three days and was as abortive as the previous ones. The High Court petition had been settled, but the papers had not arrived in Jamshedpur so we were unable to proceed with the trial. In order to expedite matters, our lawyer had made a compromise with the prosecution. It was better, he said, for there to be several separate trials rather than no trial at all, and there was such a backlog of petitions waiting to be heard in the High Court that there was no point in delaying matters further by contesting the petition. I did not care how many trials there were, as long as they started soon, so that I could stay in one place.

The trial date was set once more, this time for 28 April.

# 13. Last Transfer

Despite all the delays that year, at least I had the feeling that something was happening. Though I pretended not to care and acted as if the whole of my life were to be spent in jail, I hoped without daring to admit that I was hoping. I tried to carry on with some programmes of study between court appearances, and these helped me to push the case and its surrounding uncertainties into the back of my mind. My co-defendants often asked me questions about Britain, the Irish question, the Labour Government and the standard of living. Their thirst for information also helped to inspire me to continued mental effort.

In jail as well as outside, life was marked by a never-ending series of religious festivals. I saw these as a welcome break from the usual monotony of our daily routine. That year, some of the younger women suggested that on the Holi festival which falls in the Spring, at the end of the Hindu year, we should organize a feast and, instead of cooking and eating in small groups as we usually did, ask the warder for a big fire and some pots and pans and all cook together. Only a few prisoners were unwilling to participate; they had children outside and, understandably, did not think it right to enjoy themselves when they were not even sure if their children had enough to eat.

Having fixed a date for the celebration, we had to make sure that there were no quarrels among prisoners before that day, which might make somebody refuse to join in. This was easier said than done. The hot weather and dry winds that raged every day from morning till late afternoon seemed to put us on edge, and tempers got hotter in proportion to the weather itself. In our yard were two flowering trees that the Superintendent in one of his more benign moments had had planted to replace those that had been chopped down. I loved their big red windmill-like blossoms that appeared in the month of April. But the other women were not at all happy about the choice of tree. They called it the *jhogrela ful*, the quarrelsome flower, and insisted that, as long as the tree was in bloom, there would be dissension among those who saw its flowers. I assumed that it was because the tree blossoms in the season of hot winds that naturally hot tempers were put down to its evil properties.

The hot wind drove piles of dust and sand through our open bars and littered our cell with leaves and debris. The main blast came at about two every afternoon. For a few minutes the whole cell was filled with swirling sand that got into our eyes, ears, throats and nostrils. When it subsided, the cell we had cleaned in the morning looked as if a whirlwind had struck it. It was during this season that I most appreciated Dulali's qualities. Every evening she patiently fetched several buckets of water, shook out all the blankets, clothes and books and washed the whole cell till there was not a speck of dust left. If she had not been there, I would never have had the energy to do it, nor the patience even to stand by the trickling tap waiting for the bucket to fill. The wind left me exhausted and irritated, unable almost to think in any coherent way. By the time the evening calm arrived my temples were pounding fit to burst. Dulali on the other hand seemed quite unaffected. Quick of movement, used to hard work in every type of weather, she never so much as complained of a headache.

Following the initial interest shown in me by the Jesuit priest in Jamshedpur, I was visited from time to time by several other priests and nuns from the various mission schools and colleges. I was embarrassed by their gifts and their praise of my 'courage', feeling that I could give them little satisfaction of any kind. Although there was a world of difference between us, and though I did not find their work relevant to India's problems, I respected their sincerity. Their schools, as far as I could see, were mainly educating an English-speaking elite which, as a result of the years spent in these institutions, would be quite out of touch with the rest of the population. Moreover, it was impossible for them to operate without becoming involved in the general corruption. One priest admitted to me that, in order to ensure regular food supplies to his school, they had to take on the sons of local government officials as pupils.

One very hot day I was called to the office to meet two nuns, one Swiss, the other Austrian. Their scrubbed and shining faces and serene expressions were strangely out of keeping with the surroundings. Sitting there in the office under the portraits of distinguished former prisoners, sipping coffee and eating cakes provided by the Superintendent's wife, I felt as if I were several thousand miles and not just a few yards away from the hot dusty road and the parched fields of Hazaribagh. I had the impression that if I walked to the window I would see a view of mountain pastures and ice-capped peaks. They seemed completely unaffected by the sixty years that, between them, they had spent in India. The books on Alpine flowers and Swiss resorts they had brought for me further reinforced this impression. Though I thought their lack of passion and unwavering cheerfulness rather out of keeping with reality, I sincerely appreciated their kindness in visiting me.

When I returned from the office that afternoon, a prisoner who had recently joined us, a washerwoman by caste, and not very well liked among the other women because of her pessimism and prophecies of the bad luck that was to befall them, beckoned to me in a conspiratorial way. Wondering what the matter was, I went over to the corner where she was seated in a huddle with several other women. Motioning to me to sit down, she secretively whispered: 'Didi, do you know how to do abortions?' I was flabbergasted. Though many strange requests had come my way, this was the first time I had been asked to perform that particular task. Assuring her that I had not the slightest idea about such matters, I inquired as to whom the abortion was for. She pointed to Alamoni, a thin, sickly young woman, whom, from her lassitude and general pallor, I had already suspected to be pregnant. Alamoni's husband had been killed in a fight allegedly after taking part in robbing a rich farmer. She and her companion Radhamoni had been arrested after the incident.

The washerwoman had persuaded Alamoni that when she left jail nobody in her village would believe that the child was her dead husband's; they would assume that she had conceived in jail, and throw her out of the village. It was the general belief that jail was an iniquitous place where women could not keep their chastity and, though I never came across anything that might confirm this, Alamoni was only too easily convinced by the other woman's predictions. Moreover, she really did not want the child. She had no idea how she was going to support it now that her husband was dead, and she already had two children at home. She had decided that an abortion was the only way out. I told her to dismiss the thought; in jail there were no facilities for such operations. But she seemed to have made up her mind not to have the child. She just stopped eating, hoping that weakness would make her miscarry.

Our long-planned Holi celebration marked a new stage in relations between the women prisoners. The Sunday before the chosen date, we fasted and pooled our resources; we had flour, molasses, potatoes, mustard oil and spices. After a morning spent cooking potato curry and *puri*, a kind of deep-fried pancake, we sat in a big circle under the margosa tree and ate together. Though the food was better than most of us had eaten for months, what pleased me most was the fact that for the first time we had managed to organize and execute a programme in complete unison. The atmosphere of harmony, the mingling of so many different types and castes, the overcoming of so many inhibitions and prejudices, even if only for a short time, was something quite unique in my jail experience.

On 28 April we could not be taken to Jamshedpur because, in ironic contrast with our unity inside jail, Hindu-Muslim riots were taking place in Hazaribagh, and all available police were engaged in quelling them. April was always a bad month for riots; shortly after Holi a Muslim festival coincided with a Hindu one and there were usually bigots waiting to stir up trouble among rival groups of devotees. Many arrests were made; the ward on one side of ours was filled with Hindus and that on the other with Muslims, both shouting their own slogans. That time there was no indication of how long the trial had been adjourned for. I was relieved not to have had to make the journey in the heat and wind.

Though the Jayprakash Narayan movement had subsided, striking school teachers and factory workers took the place of the Movement détenus. One day, a girl of about seventeen was carried in with gunshot wounds in head, shoulders, back and legs. She was a colliery worker, a matriculate of a mission college forced to take whatever work she could find because her family could not afford to educate her any further. Though women had long since been prohibited from working on the actual coal face, they still carried the heavy baskets of coal on their heads, up from the mine to waiting trucks. The thought of that frail girl, little more than a child, carrying loads of coal on her head, astounded me. I wondered where she found the strength. I asked her how she had been injured.

She said the workers at her mine, dissatisfied with the 'official' union, had formed their own alternative association; once or twice they had gone on strike for improved wages and living conditions. Their quarters were one-roomed corrugated iron hovels, and there was no proper water supply. She had been earning only four rupees a day, and rice still cost over three rupees a kilogram. One night some leaders of the 'official', Congress-backed union, accompanied by a band of their men, had called the workers out of their huts. There had been a street battle, and police had arrived to break it up. Seven people, all members of the workers' own union, had been injured in firing. They, and some other union members, had been arrested for causing an affray.

Though I was by now accustomed to delays in my trial, I often wondered what my parents must be feeling. I could picture them looking forward to each new court date with the hope that my trial was really going to start. How could they have any idea of the hundred and one eventualities that might cause it to be postponed again? Their letters, on the other hand, were filled with concern for me. They were afraid that I might not be able to stand the strain of repeated postponements. The fact that, despite all the years in jail, my family and friends had not abandoned me, made a considerable impression on the jail staff. It made some of them think that I must be somebody important. One of the Special Branch men once asked a High Commission official if I was related to a very eminent family, implying that, if this was not the case, he could not understand why people were bothering about me.

One day I read in *The Times* that the Haldane Society of Lawyers had written to Mrs Gandhi protesting at the delays in bringing me to trial. Soon afterwards, the Chief Head Warder told me that the BBC World Service had broadcast news of my imprisonment. I knew that sooner or later the efforts my friends and family were making would have an effect and that the trial would really start. However, I was sceptical about the outcome; I thought that perhaps, in order to justify having kept me for so long, the authorities would contrive to find me guilty. The threat of a twenty-year sentence had, after all, been made more than once.

On 10 May 1975, the Chief Head Warder told me that I was to be ready to go to Jamshedpur at eight the next morning. At about ten a.m. on the following day, I was still waiting, lying on a blanket, surrounded by the worn khaki bags and the cardboard boxes that contained my clothes and books, when one of the children came running to call me: '*Mousi*, Alamoni's baby is falling.' As there was no privacy whatsoever in jail, even the children knew who was menstruating, who was pregnant, and now were spectators to Alamoni's miscarriage. I ran to the dormitory where Alamoni was groaning in a corner, her legs bent apart, heels pressing hard on the floor, while one woman massaged her stomach and another her shoulders, in an effort to encourage the foetus to emerge. She was deathly pale, sweating and moaning, and I could not bear to watch her in such pain. I kept going away and coming back again, not wanting to leave her yet overwhelmed by giddiness and nausea at the sight of her. I tried to tie her lank hair back, but another woman stopped me, saying that this would encourage the child to get tied up in her womb and delay the passage still longer. About an hour later, the three-month foetus appeared, and was pushed to the side of the dormitory, where it remained till the sweeper could be called to dispose of it. Alamoni was rubbed with oil and covered with blankets, to rest and recover from her ordeal. By the time the doctor arrived, it was all over.

At three o'clock the same afternoon, we were all in the dormitory. The wind was battering the broken wooden shutter and driving flurries of sand through the torn sacks hung across the bars. Drifts of sand lay here and there across the dormitory. Prokash's mother was sitting tailor-style, her crippled leg stretched grotesquely across the dingy quilt she was sewing from pieces of rag and knotted thread she had accumulated from her many sources. Beside her, old Birsi was squatting bare-breasted, picking the lice from her tattered blouse. Further down, Dulali and Kormi lay sleeping, heads covered against the sand, coutless flies crawling up their legs and across their coarse jail sarees, leaving a pattern of black specks on the white cloth. In the centre of the dormitory, Budhni was sitting on her haunches in front of the coal fire she had lit in an old oil tin, trying to shield it from the blasts of wind so she could cook her *chapatis* for the evening meal. Sweat was flowing from her forehead and the nape of her neck, marking her blue blouse navy. Some of the children were playing with the toys they had fashioned from mud and dried in the sun: miniature pots and pans, dolls and animals. Old Guruwari, the matine, was snoring beneath her coverlet, while the wardress on duty lay on the wooden bed relishing her daily massage. 'Granny' Basiran, Budhni's mother-in-law, was wheezing after her latest coughing fit, her body dry and brittle with age and toil. Savitri too was resting, alarmed and anxious; for the third day she had coughed up big clots of blood. Beside me, Santi, one of the young prisoners, was embroidering a scarf for one of her boyfriends among the convicts, a 'trusty' who had access to cloth and thread from the stores. She was watched by Satya, twelve years old, bored and lonely. I lay stretched out on Santi's home-made quilt, head propped on a makeshift pillow Satya had considerately placed behind my neck, reading a pamphlet on Ireland that had somehow run the blockade of censorship, devouring this little nourishment from the outside world. Prokash was kneeling by my feet, massaging them with oil and cracking my toe joints in imitation of his elders. On my left, Alamoni lay restless and groaning. Her hair flowed damp and tangled with oil and exertion. Radhamoni was gently rubbing her wrists and palms in an effort to induce some warmth into her thin body, cold while we were all restless from the heat and dryness. A fetid smell emerged from beneath her thin blankets. The whole dormitory was heavy with dust and the odours of mustard and coconut oil, perspiration, urine and cooking.

We were unusually quiet that day; pensive, perhaps, after Alamoni's pain. Even the children were not running and shrieking with the frenzy the wind seemed to drive them to. The hot afternoon gave us a peculiar sense of freedom. Secure in the knowledge that no warder would venture to our cloister in that merciless sun, we relaxed, sarees tucked above our knees, careless of propriety. At four o'clock the younger women would start combing and braiding their hair in a variety of styles, vermilion their partings, blacken their eyes and smooth their sarees for the day's main event, when, just before dusk, a few male prisoners would enter our precincts with the evening lentils and curry, and tablets for the sick.

Suddenly, the bell outside the gate rang commandingly. Hurriedly the wardress sat up, dragging her saree round her in an attempt to hide her naked breasts and cover her head as decency and duty demanded. Manua, her favourite, shook old Guruwari to waken her. Sleepily, the matine staggered barefoot across the burning sand towards the gate, to peer through the chink and find out what urgent message had violated our afternoon's peace.

'Mary Tyler is to go to Jamshedpur.'

'What, now?'

'Yes, right away. Tell her to hurry.'

Guruwari ran back to tell me the news. I was startled; the wardress who came on duty at midday had already told me that no police could be found to escort us to Jamshedpur that day. Now I had to be ready to go within fifteen minutes. My few belongings were swiftly packed again. Santi combed and plaited my hair, while Dulali and Kormi tied up my khaki bags with string. Budhni came running with her evening *chapatis*; she put them down on an aluminium plate in front of me.

'You must eat, Didi. You'll be hungry.'

'So will you if I eat your supper.'

'No, Didi, I've got some more. You must eat these, it's a long journey.'

Manua was foraging for the little bit of sugar she had stored against an emergency. She stirred it in a tumbler of cool water from the pitcher and brought it to me.

'Drink this sherbet, Didi. It's so hot and dry, you'll be thirsty in the jeep.'

The children were around me, fingering and smoothing my saree, clutching my hands with their clammy little fingers.

'When are you coming back, *Mousi*?'

'Oh, in a few days' time. You know how they keep taking me back and forth. I'm sure the trial won't start this time either, so I'll soon be seeing you again.'

But this was to be the last time. Today I was leaving them for ever.

Somehow, Hari over in the stores had heard that I was going. On the pretext of asking the wardress something, he came to the chink in the gate and rang the bell hesitantly. Even from inside the dormitory we could recognize his dusty face through the patched wooden planks. Everyone understood that he had come to say good-bye to me. I went to the gate alone.

'*Didi*, I heard you're going?'

'Yes, I'm off again. There's really no point in going, but I suppose I must. I'll die in this heat in that open jeep. The government's still trying to kill me off, it seems. But we have to be able to put up with all kinds of hardships, don't we? I could, of course, refuse to go. It's just another wasted journey.'

'No, *Didi*, you must go, for the sake of the others. It may cause more delays if you don't. One has to make sacrifices for the good of others.'

He knew, of course, because that was why he was in prison.

That day I said good-bye to Hari, Dulali and Kormi and all my dear companions and children, certain that I should soon be returning. But within two months, I would be in England, and they would be with me only as thoughts, memories, sleeping and waking dreams.

# 14.  A Ticket to London

Bina and I liked to plan surprises for each other. That time I was particularly looking forward to seeing her; I had managed to save four rupees by selling my rations and had bought a yard of cloth and made her a blouse. Leoni had given me some chillies, garlic and coriander leaves from the garden for her. Bina never ate the lentils and potato curry that were served up with our rice; all she needed to accompany it were some salt and a chilli or two or a little chutney.

During my absence, she had made a beautiful mud hearth. The yard at the back of my cell had once been used as a dump for coal dust, and she had dug through it, saving all the tiny pieces of coal she could find. Mixed with mud, kneaded into balls and dried in the sun, they made very effective fuel. From old pieces of wood and tin she dug up she had made some kitchen gadgets, a sieve, a board for making noodles, a stirring spoon. She had saved the few grains of wheat and barley that were always to be found in the morning chick peas, and accumulated enough to grind a couple of pounds of flour in the millstone that was kept in the female ward for the women to grind spices and flour for the staff. All Bina's preparations were for me: she was going to make me some village dishes to vary our usual indigestible diet.

Her resourcefulness never ceased to surprise me. If I ever mentioned anything we needed, she would not respond immediately. Sometimes she did not even mention the subject for days, then, quite suddenly, appeared before me with the required article. In this way we acquired nails and pegs to hang our possessions on the walls out of the way of rats, gadgets to scare the birds away from our tiny garden, and numerous other useful items. She put aside all the little tufts of thread and string dropped by the sparrows that had made their nests in the eaves of my cell, and one day presented me with a beautifully neat and strong washing line she had plaited for me. Even though we lived at such close quarters, I seldom knew how or where she had found the things she gave me. There was nothing sinister about it; she just kept her eyes open and wasted nothing that could possibly be of use. Since childhood she had been used to relying on her own skill and ingenuity and it came naturally to her.

Thursday 15 May arrived. I had been dreading the thought of going to court, which always entailed a long wait in the stifling police van. Now we were at the height of the hot season and the heat and humidity were intense. Despite the judge's order, in response to our protests – that we were to be given access to a sufficiently ventilated room with toilet facilities and drinking water while waiting to be taken into court – the police kept us in the same crowded vehicle as before. The wardress who always accompanied me was not allowed to leave my side for a moment. The two of us sat cramped in the seat next to the driver's, our sarees clinging to our damp bodies, heads aching from the lack of air and the sun burning on the windscreen, unable to stretch our legs or even get a glass of water without a tiresome process of request and explanation to one of the policemen on duty round the van. It was, of course, far worse for the men in the back of the van.

Visits to court were always accompanied by guards from three separate police forces: black-bereted armed constabulary, green-bereted military police, red-bereted regular police. They were as bored with the whole proceedings as we were, but at least they could stand out in the open air under the trees, leaning on their rifles and chatting desultorily, occasionally stopping to order away any curious onlooker who came too near the van. Like the jail staff, they adorned their rumpled uniforms with motley additions of dingy white plimsolls, knotted scarves and handkerchiefs. Some wore belts, others let their shirts hang loosely outside their khaki shorts. Nearly all were unshaven and unkempt.

That day, there was one encouraging development: the judge ordered that we were now to remain in Jamshedpur, as witnesses were being called and there were no further obstacles to the trial's commencing. I was elated at the thought of settling in one place again at last. I would be able to sort out my books and papers, organize a programme of study and help Bina with her reading again. When I got back, we set about making the cell as pleasant as possible. Bina had managed to get hold of some whitewash from a warder and next morning we whitewashed the place inside and out. The Consul now in charge of my case had obligingly brought me a variety of plastic bags to protect my books and clothing. Though they were printed with such incongruities as 'Mothercare' and 'Selfridges', they lent a cheerful aspect to the white walls. Strange as it now seems to me, I was far more interested in making my surroundings as attractive as I was able than in the prospect of the trial's starting.

Two days later, shortly after our midday meal, I was summoned to the office. It was unusual for anybody to disturb us at that hour, when most people were resting. I re-wound the saree I had loosened for comfort in the afternoon heat, and was taken directly to the Superintendent himself. I could see from his face that something was wrong. He motioned to the telephone: the Deputy High Commission in Calcutta had just phoned to tell him that my mother had died on Thursday, 15 May. Though the news itself came as a shock, it was something that had been in the back of my mind all my five years in jail. My mother had been a heart patient for a long time and I had often wondered whether she would be able to stand all the strain. Now the moment I had been dreading had come. I went straight back to my cell, not wanting to cry in front of jail officers.

As I walked through the gate, Bina came to me, questioningly, wondering why I had been called to the office. As I started to tell her, I was no longer able to prevent the tears from flowing. Only a day or two previously I had received my mother's letter, full of concern for me, not mentioning her own physical condition, just encouraging me not to worry and to stay optimistic. Now she was gone. Bina took my hand and led me gently to the water tap. Making me sit down on the concrete slab beside it, she poured mug after mug of soothing cool water over my hot head and burning limbs. For a long time she did not speak; then she started quietly encouraging me to be brave, and to remember the millions of people who daily suffered pain and torment as great as mine. I was not alone. And I must remember that, for those who wanted to help others, there could be no hot or cold, no personal joy or sorrow, no easy or hard; everything had to be accepted and borne without flinching.

After the initial shock, I lapsed into cynicism, hating those who had caused my uninvolved and innocent parents so much agony. I felt bitter, frustrated and helpless. I kept thinking about my father, left with the double burden of my mother's death and my imprisonment. But I could not even send him a telegram. I longed to see him and my sister for just an hour to comfort them. I knew they would be worrying about how I had taken the news. My letter to him was kept the usual fortnight in the local Police Office before being posted. To make matters worse, on 29 May, the next court date, I was refused permission, for the first time, to meet the consul who came to see me. I was impatient to hear how my mother had died and to send a message to my father, but it had to wait. Nothing, it seemed, could evoke a human response from the bureaucrats who controlled my life. It was lucky that I had Bina and the others to turn to.

Insects and vermin had always been a problem in both Hazaribagh and Jamshedpur. Now that my kitten was dead I noticed a tremendous increase in the rat population. At night I was sometimes woken by a rat running across my bare flesh. Once I felt one nibbling my toe. Another night, the noise of a tin rattling broke my sleep. Four rats had somehow prised off the lid of my molasses tin and were devouring the contents. They ruined everything they could get their teeth into. Several times I had bad dreams about giant rats. Every time I asked the authorities to get me a trap, they laughed, as if I were slightly eccentric. When the British Consul next came to see me, in mid-June, I surprised him with the request to buy me a rat-trap from the bazaar with my own money. It was probably the strangest request he had heard from a prisoner, but he obliged. Within a week I had caught seventeen fat rats, and there were plenty more around.

At about the same time, there was an innovation in the jail. Our cells were fitted with electric lights. The Superintendent was very proud of this achievement; it did not occur to him that it would do nothing at all to alleviate prisoners' conditions. A few days previously, the Jailer had written to the Minister for Jails explaining that he was allowing the old and very sick prisoners to sleep outside on the verandahs, to avoid suffocation in the wards. If anything, the electric light made matters worse than before. The lights were controlled from a central switch and left on all night. The naked bulb glaring in our eyes seemed to make the hot nights hotter still; I also felt deprived of the welcome solitude I had enjoyed in the darkness after locking.

Our trial was now to start on 23 June. Not long before that day, the newspaper carried a long report about Hadiabad, a village in Bhojpur district that had been burned to the ground by a party of landlords and their men, in retaliation for the Harijan villagers' having allegedly given shelter to Naxalites. The fourteen-year-old son of one of the villagers who was himself said to be a Naxalite, was hacked to pieces because the landlords were unable to find his father. Not a single one of the attackers had been arrested, though several of their names were printed in the paper.

The start of the trial was an anti-climax. The great event we had waited for so long, when it came, was dull and boring. Proceedings were quite undramatic, and from the beginning it was obvious that it was all going to take a very long time. As each witness came to the stand, the Judge noted down all his statements laboriously in longhand. The Prosecution had produced a list of nearly a hundred witnesses, all but one or two of them police, to be called in each separate trial.

The whole scene struck me as Kafkaesque: standing at the back of the court, I was unable even to hear what the black-robed judge and the penguin-like lawyers in their black gowns and white starched collars were saying. When I complained that the proceedings were inaudible, the prosecution accused me of deliberately disrupting and delaying the trial! Protests were of no avail, the goings-on at the front of the court continued to be inaudible, and only a few of the keenest of the defendants sat as far forward as possible, on an old carpet that had been found for the occasion, straining their ears to try to understand what was happening.

I stayed at the back, observing the scene as if from outside, while my fate was decided by ghostly and remote figures whose lips moved but whose voices were but faint echoes. Those of the accused who had given up trying to hear sat, like naughty school-boys, one playing patience, some chewing chick peas, some surreptitiously flicking them at the others in front, one or two dozing, others reading newspapers, one sneaking the handkerchief out of the pocket of the boy next to him. It was hard to believe that matters of life and death were being decided. One could almost have been back in the classroom, except that the court was surrounded by armed guards and there was a bayonet within a yard of my nose. By that time I was so used to the presence of armed police everywhere I went that I hardly noticed them. But, as soon as each day's hearing finished, even before the Judge had turned, with a swish of robes, and left the court, they closed in on us with ropes and handcuffs, to string the men together for return to jail.

In another part of India, recent court proceedings were having far-reaching consequences. Shortly before the start of our trial, the Allahabad High Court had found the Prime Minister, Mrs Indira Gandhi, guilty of corrupt election practices. Her conviction, coming on the same day as news of the Congress Party's defeat in the Gujarat elections, was a serious blow for the government. Opposition parties demanded her resignation. But, far from responding to this call, on 26 June 1975, Mrs Gandhi declared a state of emergency in the country and set about arresting both leaders and activists of opposition parties. Even before the news reached me, on the night of 26 June I heard the sound of heavy vehicles drawing up outside the jail. With my usual optimism, I imagined that perhaps Amalendu, Kalpana and the others were being brought back from Calcutta. Next morning I was told that the trucks had in fact carried newly arrested opponents of the government. That day, for the last time, the papers were able to report details of the arrests. After the imposition of censorship laws, they contained little but ministerial speeches and adulation of the Prime Minister.

A couple of days later, the Naxalite block was subjected to a sudden dawn search. The same morning, I was told not to take a pen or newspaper to court. I demurred, explaining that I intended to spend the hours sitting in the police van doing a crossword puzzle. In the end the Jailer relented. Though these incidents were undoubtedly the result of the emergency, they represented to us nothing but an intensification of the arbitrary and high-handed dealings to which we had long been accustomed. Mrs Gandhi's need to impose a state of emergency to deal with the opposition in the country was a significant indication of her government's weakness. What intrigued me was that the Soviet Union, a country which was supposedly concerned with the well-being of the world's oppressed people, could, as on previous occasions, declare its all-out support for the action of the Indian Government.

From the time I had first come to Jamshedpur in 1973, I had lodged repeated complaints with the authorities about the leaking roof of my cell. Even if there was a slight rain shower, the water came straight through the ceiling. Note had been taken of my grievance, and Public Works Department officials of varying degrees of seniority had come at least a dozen times to inspect, measure and take a decison on what was to be done. In the end, we had patched the roof up ourselves with a mixture of cowdung, tar and cement. Now, at last, a bricklayer and three labourers appeared to repair it. Unfortunately, I could not attribute this development to the efficiency Mrs Gandhi's emergency was said to have inspired, because the date had apparently been arranged several weeks before. The warder objected to the presence in the group of two women labourers; the bricklayer said they were essential to the work: no man would fetch and carry sand and cement. I was interested to hear that the two women, doing the heaviest work, were earning less than either of the men.

A week after the trial started, one of our fellow accused contracted typhoid. Proceedings were halted for a couple of days until he was able to sign his consent to the hearing's continuing in his absence. Another boy submitted a petition for two days' parole to visit his old father, dying of liver cancer. It was refused. A day or two later, a telegram arrived to inform him of the old man's death.

On the morning of Friday, 4 July 1975, my lawyer beckoned to me as I entered the court. He whispered that the case against me was to be withdrawn. I asked 'Which case?' thinking that maybe the prosecution had decided not to proceed with the picric acid charge, about which there had been some debate the previous day. Mr Mishra amazed me by saying, 'All the cases.' The Prosecution was preparing a petition for withdrawal of all charges against me. Due to this new development, the hearing was adjourned until the next morning.

The following day the petition was duly submitted. The Prosecution had decided to withdraw the case 'on grounds of inexpediency'. I did not even notice the peculiar wording, drafted by a lawyer sent specially from Delhi for the occasion, until the High Commission secretary present at the hearing pointed it out to me. The wording was hastily amended. Now I was to be acquitted on 'grounds of expediency', because my further detention would be prejudicial to the good relations between two Commonwealth countries, India and Britain. The Judge remarked that these grounds were very weak. However, he had heard nothing in the evidence so far adduced to make him object to the petition. He called me to the witness stand and said: 'You are acquitted of all charges. Go and be happy.' I said: 'How is it possible to be happy with so many people still held in jail without trial?' He smiled, kindly. Perhaps he understood.

Lawyers, accused and press correspondents thronged round to congratulate me. The police tried to restrain them. Journalists were asking me about my immediate plans. 'It's not over yet,' I said. They were puzzled. But I knew that, even after so many years of detention, the Indian Government would not release me unconditionally, particularly at this crucial juncture in the nation's history. I was right. I returned to the jail with the other accused, as usual. At the gate, I was prevented from leaving the van. The wardress was weeping silently beside me. She had been appointed specially to guard me, and knew that her job had now come to an end and she had to find some other way to feed and educate her four children. For her, extreme financial insecurity and fear of what was to come had turned the happy occasion of my release into a tragedy. In fact, after serving three years, she was entitled to permanent status, but she had been deliberately laid off for two days shortly before the completion of the statutory period and then reappointed. The two days she had not worked would be counted as a break in service. By the use of this ploy every three years, a person could be prevented from ever being employed on a permanent basis. This ensured that he or she could be made redundant at a moment's notice with no redress.

As the men disappeared inside the jail, a police officer wearing a peaked cap and jack-boots presented me with a deportation order. I was instructed to leave the country within seven days. The order was dated 17 June and signed by the Joint Secretary to the Government of India. I was ordered back inside the jail. In theory, I was 'free', but the police had made all necessary preparations. Another warrant for my arrest had been issued, charging me with travelling without a valid document. The passport the police had confiscated after my arrest was still in their possession.

The British Consul came to see me after seeing the local Superintendent of Police. A plane ticket to England had been booked for the next day. I was to leave at dawn the following morning to go to Calcutta. He would accompany me that far.

Back in my cell, I tried to talk to Bina, while numerous other women crowded round us. I was telling her that she must continue with her study, must not become depressed, even though I was far away I would not forget her. I would write to her, and, who knew, perhaps one day we would meet again.

That night I did not sleep. I was worried in case my notes and diaries should be confiscated. I racked my brains trying to think of a way to smuggle them out. They were too bulky to hide. In the end, I hit on a plan. I carefully went through them, changing the word 'Indian' to 'British' everywhere I had made a critical comment on the government, so that a casual reader would imagine I was referring to the British Government. I changed Mrs Gandhi's name to 'Mrs Thatcher' or 'The Queen' and wrote religious titles on the inside cover of each book. I thought that would do the trick if the Special Branch decided to be difficult.

Next morning, the wardress called me at four o'clock. It was still dark and I had not finished bathing when she came back and told me to hurry up and get dressed, someone wanted to see me. A friendly warder had kept a promise he had made me secretly the day before. One of the men in my case, his eyes still half closed with sleep, had been brought to see me before the Special Branch arrived on duty. I had wanted this last chance of explaining to the others what had happened after they left me in the police van, because I knew that the authorities would not tell them and I wanted them to hear the story undistorted. When I told him that I was being deported, he smiled wistfully and said, 'Don't forget us.' Then, as he turned to leave, he looked back, raised his fist in a salute and added: 'We shall meet again. We shall. Definitely.'

Within a few minutes I had to say good-bye to Bina, Heera, old Gulabi and the others. The children came to be kissed. Raju, Heera's son, was saying, '*Didi, Didi*.' The warder urged me to hurry. All I could say to Bina was: 'Don't fret. Take care of your health.' We were both crying.

The Superintendent and Jailer had got up early to say good-bye to me. They ordered tea from the near-by stall. The police escort had already arrived and the British Consul was waiting. Together we climbed into the truck that was to take us to the station. Nobody attempted to search or question me. At the railway station, the Bihar Joint Secretary for Home was waiting with the Superintendent of Police. They conducted us to the first-class air-conditioned coach of the express train that was to take us all to Calcutta. Soon we were speeding through the flat and beautiful countryside of Bengal. The paddy was a foot high in the fields; banana trees, bamboo thickets, ponds, mud houses, sometimes a village and a small railway station, passed by as if on film. I was thinking how much I loved this country. We chatted and drank coffee. One of the policewomen accompanying us had her little girl with her, a thin and weak-looking child. She looked questioningly at me, not understanding why a 'mem-sahib' needed an armed police guard.

At Howrah Station, I was handed over to Calcutta police. The Consul promised to see me again at the airport. Accompanied by three plain-clothes police officers, I was driven in a saloon car through the filthy haze of Calcutta. Amalendu and Kalpana were within a few miles of me. Did they know that I was going? I had asked the British official to get permission for me to see Amalendu and his family before leaving, but he said he was sure it would not be granted. I asked the police for the return of my watch and money that had been taken from Amalendu's house when I was arrested. They produced only my passport, saying that I should have told them 'before' about the other things – as if they had given me any warning that I should be leaving India so abruptly.

At the airport I was conducted with great politeness to an air-conditioned Domestic VIP suite. I was to make myself comfortable and have a good rest. My plane would be leaving around midnight. It was not yet noon. The policeman left, telling me that I was to remember that I was no longer a prisoner, but a guest. A trapped guest: they locked the door behind them. A few minutes later there was a knock. The policemen again. Would I mind if two of them sat in the room with me? I objected. I was not going to lie down and go to sleep in front of them. They went away again. Ten minutes later, an airport policewoman arrived. She was no more than twenty. She smiled nervously and sat on the sofa inside the door. I dozed off, but woke up shivering in the unaccustomed cool of the air-conditioning. A waiter brought me chicken and ice-cream. They kept urging me to eat and drink more. I was to have anything I liked. One of the plain-clothes men reappeared from time to time for a friendly chat. Would I contact his relatives in England? Did I know Mr Das of London?

Later in the day, the Deputy High Commissioner himself came to see me. He was pleasant and courteous, but made his point several times: I was not thinking of returning to India, was I? He hoped not. Five years was a long time. A couple of high-ranking police officers came to take their leave. One advised me to wait for a year or so before coming back to India. By then, he said, Amalendu would have been released.

Later that evening, the local Reuter correspondent and another journalist arrived to interview me. I was not at all keen, but probably they had made some 'arrangement' with the plain-clothes man, because he urged me to meet them for a few minutes. They came in, looking like Laurel and Hardy. Had I changed my political views after five years in jail? No. I was still an advocate of violent revolution, then? I told them not to put words in my mouth. Getting little joy from the interview, they departed. I never discovered how they had managed to break the top secrecy of the operation and find out about my presence at Dum Dum Airport.

The Consul returned with a suitcase. My possessions were still in khaki bags. He had also, kindly, brought a few sweets for my sister's children, and a pair of shoes and tennis socks. I thought my flimsy sandals might not be suitable for the English climate, even in July. I changed my saree for the only European clothes I had, the smock I had made myself and an old pair of baggy trousers. The consul's wife came with a big bouquet of flowers. They were pleased for me, perhaps more than I was for myself. I kept thinking about Amalendu and his family, wondering if by some miracle they might find out that I was going and turn up to see me off. I ate again, vegetable curry this time. I could not face any more meat.

At last, it was a quarter to midnight. They took me down to the VIP exit. The Bihar Joint Secretary for Home was there again, together with many of those people who had come to see me during the day. They stood in a line, politely shook my hand, wished me all the best, smiled courteously. Two of the plain-clothes men accompanied me right out to the plane and did not leave me until I was safely up the gangway, clutching the ticket and boarding pass that had been given to me.

A British Airways plane. Another sign of courtesy? A steward was whispering in my ear. Would I like a small brandy on the airlines? No, I would not. I had not touched alcohol for years, and did not think I could take it. Half past midnight. They started serving roast chicken and Brussels sprouts. The very thought of it made me want to vomit. Did the other passengers know who I was? Was everyone looking at me? No. The four-teen-hour journey was tormentingly monotonous. The Bengali doctor next to me was taking his sick father to England for treatment. He started asking me about my stay in India. How long had I been there? Where? Doing what? I said he would be surprised if I told him the truth. Was I Miss Tyler? He had guessed as much. He had read about me in the newspaper.

Stewardesses plied us non-stop with orange juice, continental breakfast, coffee, English breakfast. I could not eat half of it. My fellow-passengers were munching away. There was little else to do. A steward started selling duty-free drink and tobacco. I had five pounds the Consul had given me. I might as well buy something. I could still save enough for my fare from Heathrow if nobody came to meet me. I nervously asked for two hundred cigarettes and half a bottle of whisky. It was the first direct com-mercial transaction I had performed for over five years.

What was Amalendu doing? Did he know? Would they know in London that I was coming?

Heathrow. The steward whispered to me to stay on the plane till the other passengers left. Ten minutes later, my father was there, clutching me, sobbing. My sister with the two-year-old daughter I had never seen. We walked towards passport control. Press photographers surrounded us, cameras clicking and flash-ing. All I could think of was the amount of film they were wasting. 'Smile, please. Hold the baby's hand. Hug your dad. Put your arm round your sister. That's it.'

Everyone was surprised to see that my passport was still in order. Had I been vaccinated? Yes, several times, but I had no certificate. Another vaccination, then. Down to a room where a press conference had been set up. Blinding lights. My friends, Jill with the four-year-old daughter I had read about in her letters, Ruth, hugging me. My cousin and her husband. Everyone looking enormous. Somebody hung a microphone round my neck and the questions started. My father came up to me, advised by a Foreign Office official to tell me to cut it short.

At last we got away. My father was propelling me towards his car. Soon we were on the road to Cornwall. Apples, bananas, cheese, as much as I wanted. But through the window the green English fields I had thought about so often in India looked parched and yellow.

As I write, eight months after my release, the trial which started on 23 June 1975 drags on, interminably, for my erstwhile co-defendants. Amalendu, Kalpana, Bina and thousands of alleged Naxalites are still in jail, almost without exception in conditions far worse than mine. Some have been held without trial for seven years. Since the Emergency declared on 26 June 1975, tens of thousands of other people have been arrested and interned. Innumerable poor peasants and workers like those with whom I spent my years in prison are still being held indefinitely, waiting for their cases to be settled. Children are growing up in jail.

Amalendu's crime, Kalpana's crime, is the crime of all those who cannot remain unmoved and inactive in an India where a child crawls in the dust with a begging bowl; where a poor girl can be sold as a rich man's plaything; where an old woman must half-starve herself in order to buy social acceptance from the powers-that-be in her village; where countless people die of sheer neglect; where many are hungry while food is hoarded for profit; where usurers and tricksters extort the fruits of labour from those who do the work; where the honest suffer while the villainous prosper; where justice is the exception and injustice the rule; and where the total physical and mental energy of millions of people is spent on the struggle for mere survival. It is the crime of those who know that a radical change is necessary, so that the skill, creativity, ingenuity and diligence of the Indian people can be given full scope to work in building a different kind of India, a truly independent India, a better India.

Indefinite incarceration, deprivation of civil liberties, intimidation and torture or, indeed, any other negative measure taken by the present or any other administration to silence those who speak out or act against the prevailing injustice and inhumanity, will not solve India's problems. As long as any government maintains an attitude of contempt for the population as a whole, as long as it rules the country by tyranny and the type of callousness that enables it to spend time debating whether a man has died from starvation or malnutrition and to differentiate between the two, India's agony will continue.

MARCH 1976

# Postscript

November 1977

The 'Emergency' regime continued for more than one and a half years after I left India. The main developments during that time are fairly widely known by now. Arbitrary arrests, accompanied in many cases by brutal torture; the withdrawal of workers' bonuses and cost of living allowances and a *de facto* ban on trade union activity; the suspension and subsequent amendment of articles of the Constitution guaranteeing basic rights; censorship, forced sterilization and other tyrannical measures deprived the Indian people as a whole of even the semblance of 'freedom' which had previously existed. An atmosphere of fear, uncertainty and intimidation prevailed.

All through this period it was extremely difficult to maintain contacts with Amalendu, his family and other friends in India. Mail was often tampered with, and people in India were afraid to write anything that might be interpreted as critical of the Congress government. I in turn was hesitant to write to them, for fear of landing them in trouble.

Even so, I received, by various routes, occasional letters from Amalendu, Kalpana, Bina and others. These courageous, resolute and affectionate letters inspired me to continue in the campaign being conducted in Britain against the outrages of the 'Emergency' in particular and on the question of political prisoners and civil rights in general. Despite all the restrictions on communication, I was delighted to see that people in India were well informed about our efforts.

Contrary to the Gandhi regime's claims and promises, for most people the 'Emergency' brought no noticeable improvement in their economic or social condition.

In January 1977, Indira Gandhi unexpectedly announced that

a General Election would be held in March. Various parliamentary opposition parties, which had been functioning underground during the 'Emergency', united to form the Janata (People's) Party; they were soon joined by some prominent defectors from Mrs Gandhi's own party. Campaigning on a platform of 'Dictatorship versus Democracy', they promised, if they came to power, the unconditional release of all political prisoners, withdrawal of the constitutional amendments and abolition of the Maintenance of Internal Security Act.

To the astonishment of many people abroad (including myself), the Janata Party won the election with a good majority, and ended thirty years of Congress Party rule. Mrs Gandhi was defeated in her own constituency, as were most of her ministers. In her final gesture as Prime Minister, she ordered the 'Emergency' to be withdrawn.

The Janata Party has now been in power for over seven months. Though there was some initial slight improvement in the general climate (the lifting of press censorship and of the ban on certain political parties, for example), so far, for the majority of Indian people, little has changed. Moreover, the preventive detention measures,* the constitutional amendments and the emergency provisions used by the previous government all remain in the Janata's political arsenal. Whether they will be abolished is still a matter of debate.

As far as political prisoners are concerned, the new government lost little time in releasing their own supporters who had been imprisoned during the 'Emergency': in contrast, they were hesitant to act in the case of Naxalite and other political prisoners who had been detained long before 1975, and many of whom had spent over seven years in prison without trial. However, under pressure from the civil liberties organizations which were emerging and growing in various parts of India, they did begin to release the people who had been held under preventive detention legislation without specific charges. But, for Amalendu,

---

* It was afterwards decided, first, to keep M I S A and, subsequently, to scrap it.

Kalpana, Bina and thousands of others said to be held 'awaiting trial', there has so far been no release. And though it seems that, under the increasing pressure of popular opinion, some state governments may release their political prisoners, there appears to be little hope at all for those who are held in states where the Congress Party is still in power at the provincial level.

It is very clear: what has happened so far is nothing like the general amnesty which the Janata Party promised in its election manifesto; and the eventual release of all political prisoners will depend on the strength and determination of the struggle being waged on their behalf.

'My' trial continued in Jamshedpur after my departure. Postponements and delays continued, but the trial was finally completed in May 1977, almost seven years to the day since the accused persons had been arrested. Of the thirty-four defendants, thirty were acquitted outright and released. Four people were sentenced for seven years on arms charges, and were released one week later, after spending the full seven years in prison.

Bina is still in Jamshedpur Prison, hoping that the Bihar state government will implement a recent amnesty decision. Kalpana and Amalendu are in Calcutta prisons, hoping that the 'Left Front' government of West Bengal will soon decide whether they qualify for release as political prisoners. Kalpana writes long, poetic and spirited letters. Amalendu's short, sometimes wistful notes do not reflect the alert, positive state of mind which, according to visitors' reports, he has been able to preserve despite all the years of suffering. Kalpana writes that she is losing her teeth, after years of dental neglect. Amalendu has had a stomach ulcer for several years now, and recently has lost consciousness several times through abdominal pain. Even if released, it seems improbable that they will fully regain their health.

The Indian government has recently granted me permission to go to India to visit Amalendu and his family. Perhaps, in the present volatile situation, it is better to make the journey sooner than later. Amalendu's old father is determined to stay alive for the day when Amalendu and I meet again. All of us are hoping that the meeting will not have to take place within prison walls.

The various facts and documents published by the civil liberties groups since the end of the Emergency (and some which were published in secret earlier) have made me realize that my own dark picture of Bengal and Bihar in the early seventies was still far too bright. Stories of torture, cold-blooded killings by police, outright murders described as 'encounters', and other gruesome happenings have come to light in considerable detail and with sufficient substantiating evidence. So far, however, little has been done to punish the people who were responsible.

In India now, people who were prisoners are ministers: 'democracy' is said to have been restored. But the Indian newspapers still report deaths from police bullets, bans on meetings and processions, atrocities against Harijans: abysmal poverty continues without sign of relief. Only now it is the Janata government which is the villain; and the Congress Party, still dominated by the presence of Indira Gandhi, has assumed the incongruous and grotesquely hypocritical role of champion of the poor and oppressed.

On the brighter side, there are the civil liberties movement, the growing political consciousness of broader sections of people, and the continuing struggle against injustice on many fronts and in many places. There is the emergence of new trade unions and peasants' organizations at the local level, and the understanding among younger people that old mistakes must not be repeated. Perhaps the present eventful period will help to develop a political leadership that can unite the truly concerned and honest elements in the population and show the way to a better future and a society which will guarantee to its members genuine rights that cannot be removed at the whim of a few individuals.

POST-POSTSCRIPT – April 1978. Amalendu and Kalpana were released in January this year. Bina was released on bail a little earlier. An unknown number of political prisoners is still in detention.

## More About Penguins
and Pelicans

# An Eye to India

*The Unmasking of a Tyranny*

David Selbourne

'I am a poor person, and India is a desert. I do not know how to arrange the facts for you. But you can let the world know what happened. It is your duty.'

The brutal truths of India's long-standing condition attained a new dimension under the 1975 'Emergency'. This book provides a moving and definitive account of the degeneration of a political system, and of the scale of assaults on the country's people and institutions.

The true nature of India's economic new deal, and of the socialism which was invoked by India's rulers, is also critically examined; and what emerges is not a renascent India, but 'politics of illusion and cruelty, of lies and violence'. *An Eye to India* is an object lesson in the analysis of ideology and political practice, both in the Third World and beyond.

# An Area of Darkness

V. S. Naipaul

Coming from a family which left India only two generations ago, V. S. Naipaul felt that his roots lay in India. But the country and its attitudes remained outside his experience, in an 'area of darkness', until, with some apprehension, he spent a year there. He arrived at Bombay, then travelled as far north as Kashmir, east to Calcutta and south to Madras, taking in a pilgrimage to a holy cave in the Himalayas and a stay on the Dal Lake. With his novelist's perception and sense of comedy he both describes the places, people and incidents, and manages to convey the meaning which lies behind them. He shares his experience of India generously and gives the reader deep insight into a country and a writer's mind.

'Tender, lyrical, explosive . . . excellent'
– John Wain

'Most compelling and vivid' – V. S. Pritchett

# The Seventh Gate

Peter Greave

'Thrilling, funny and pleasurable . . . precise and candid, *The Seventh Gate* is the story of an adventurous, action-packed, emotion-filled life, full of twists and turns, disasters and escapes, comedy and suffering, so enthralling that at times I felt it had to be fiction. Peter Greave's tale of his tempest-tossed family, headed by a mad, vain, handsome father is like that of a global *Huckleberry Finn* . . . Such gusto, passion and compassion' – Alan Brien in the *Sunday Times*

'One of the most remarkable books about life in India ever to have been written—quite superb . . . gives a picture of different aspects of Indian life in a way that Kipling would have been proud of' – David Holloway in the *Daily Telegraph*

'A marvellous book – joyous and enchanting. It is a celebration of life such as perhaps only someone who had been deprived of all that makes it worthwhile could compose. It is also a remarkable account of a childhood marked by the most extraordinary vicissitudes' – Tony Gould in *New Society*

## Prisoner of Mao

Bao Ruo-Wang and Rudolph Chelminski

In December 1957, Chinese Security Police called on Bao Ruo-Wang, a French citizen, at his home in Peking where he was arrested and taken to jail for interrogation and re-education. Convicted for counter-revolutionary activities to twelve years of 'Reform Through Labour', he was finally released in 1964, shortly after France and China had established diplomatic relations, as 'a special gesture of extraordinary magnanimity'.

Few people, among millions who experience them, have survived a sentence in the Chinese system of labour camps. None have recorded that harsh life of deprivation with the accuracy and honesty that distinguish this account. *Prisoner of Mao* is remarkable for its humanity, its hope and, above all, for its unforced recognition of the quality of Chinese communism.

'A unique and extraordinarily valuable book'
– *Daily Telegraph*